Ready, Set, 30

A tale of figuring it all out

...whatever that means

Angélique Joan

CONTENTS

INTRODUCTION

O h, hi there. Welcome. Thanks for tagging along. You're catching me on quite a day. This gal has just turned 30. I don't really understand how this has happened...Maybe it's a fluke. Maybe I'm actually still 29 and Time is wrong. That's it, Time is faulty. It's having an off day and needs a minute to catch up on people's ages and stuff...

Or maybe, and more plausibly, Time has not spared me like I hoped it would, and I have indeed reached the big 3-0... Damn it. As much as I tried to convince the Universe that turning 30 didn't feel like the appropriate course of action for me, Time surprisingly, and very rudely, did not take my feelings into consideration. Even that whole week of freaking out before my birthday, reluctantly saying goodbye to my messy, unstable, seemingly carefree twenties, didn't do the trick. Time was like: 'Na y'all, she's turning 30 and she ain't gonna complain about it.' *Time is this dude from Texas in my head, apparently.*

And so, here I am. Bloody 30.

It's funny, you never actually think it's going to happen to you, do you? Thirty seems so far away when you're a teenager – so far so that you can't even imagine it happening and you sort of live in denial that it ever will. You can look at people around you, getting older, reaching some big age milestones, and yet it doesn't really occur to you that this WILL happen to you too.

Or maybe you guys are already super aware of time and the inevitable process of ageing? Good for you. I am most certainly not. It hadn't even entered my mind a year ago.

When a few of my friends turned 30 last year, I remember thinking: 'Great, another opportunity to attend a big bash. Let's party.' Or, 'Oh, wow, can't believe they're 30 now. It really seems like they've got it all figured out. Good for them. Love it.' while I carried on eating my overpriced take-out food, watched *Friends* for the eighteenth time, *pretending I didn't know that Ross and Rachel break up 78 times in the show,* and avoided that pile of laundry on the floor. And yet, I was 29 years old; just months away from that same birthday, not even close to thinking anything of it or what it would mean for my life. *Because who hasn't used their twenties as an excuse to go about life, every day, avoiding adulthood? No? Just me? Excellent.* Thirty meant I had to start having a clue...in my head at least; thirty meant no playing around. This was serious business. *It would be nice of me to say that those 29-year-old tendencies are behind me, but take-out food and Friends are two things you simply can't take away from me. Don't fight me on this.*

That said, it's happened.

The big question now is: Does this mean I'm actually an adult now? And what on earth does *that* mean? Does it mean I have to enjoy ironing clothes and learning how to cook properly?! Fuck. If you look up the word 'Adult' in the dictionary – *or as millennials call it, Google* – here's what it says:

"An adult is a person who is fully grown and developed, a person who has responsibilities and accomplishes mundane but necessary tasks."

I have a few things to say about this. In my opinion, it is just an awful, depressing and quite inaccurate description of what an adult is. First of all, *'fully developed'*? Excuse me, my boobs are somehow still growing. *One even more than the other, might I add.* And depending on the time of year, *meaning Christmas food and my ongoing, serious relationship with chocolate,* my butt will also grow in size. *So, joke's on you, Google.*

Responsibility... such a boring word. And vague. It can mean so many different things. I understand I have a responsibility to myself... to keep myself alive. That's also called survival instinct, right? Like knowing when to eat and sleep and making sure I look both ways when I cross the street. Pretty basic. I don't think responsibility defines us as adults. Kids can easily, and very loudly, let us know when they are hungry and need sleep, and they also know not to run in the street... usually. And, as we're on the subject of children, I think we can all admit that some of them can be way more intuitive and smarter than many of the so-called adults I've encountered in life. *No offence.*

Sure, kids don't have to deal with booking the annual dentist check-up, paying the electricity bill or having to pretend to enjoy Grandma's weird gift at Christmas. They can throw tantrums and not get the relentless 'Oh, just grow up!' comment from their parents, *which I may or may not still get from mine, from time to time...* They have the luxury of being unrestricted in their behaviour and what they say at times. But, I've definitely witnessed children be more attentive, respectful, *responsible* and have more compassionate instincts than some adults I've met.

Case in point: I once saw a child, no older than five, who was sitting with his mum on the Underground in London, get up from his seat to comfort a woman who was crying opposite him. I think the whole carriage started to cry when he started patting her hand and telling her it would be ok. Very few adults would do that. Some adults just did not get the memo about compassion and kindness. I'm sure you can think of a few in your head right now, am I right?

Anyway! I diverged there for a sec.

I can't seem to pin down one specific thing responsibility could mean. Maybe it means something different to each of us and a culmination of things, too. I asked my little brother, who is 26, what he thought it meant. He told me he thought true responsibility comes when you become a parent, having to keep someone else alive. Coming from someone who isn't even a parent yet, I was impressed by this answer. But what does that mean for the many other humans who aren't parents?

For me, at this moment in time, I'd probably say responsibility is making sure I have enough money in the bank to pay rent and feed myself. *Chocolate and wine included of course – cranky wouldn't even begin to describe my state without those two essentials.* So, yeah, that would be it. Responsible enough to afford chocolate, to prevent people from having to endure my crankiness. Maybe I've got some work to do on the responsibility front, you say? You might be right. My responsibility criteria is pretty poor.

I can kind of get on board with the '*mundane and necessary tasks*' part. It's true that most people associate paying their taxes or getting a credit card with 'Welcome to Adulthood' moments. *Both of which I'm not entirely sure I'm doing properly, but let's stay in denial about that for a bit longer.* I would also say: buying furniture from Ikea, building that bloody furniture, making the bed every morning, going antique shopping and actually enjoying it, calling the doctor for an appointment, calling anyone in a professional capacity for that matter, changing a lightbulb, checking the Amazon reviews on random home products, complaining about the weather, fixing something in the house, sewing, changing a tyre and saying things like 'Go on then, let's have another cuppa'. 'There there', 'Oh, we just watched this lovely documentary about birds going extinct last night', 'Those lyrics are offensive', 'The music is too loud in here' also qualify. I have personally done and said all these things and it never even entered my mind that this might mean I was closer to adulthood than I realised.

Have you ever asked yourself what was the moment you thought you were an adult?

While writing this book, I asked a few of my friends, younger and older, when they felt they had become an adult. Every answer was different. Many of them had never even thought about the concept before I asked. I got a lot of 'What's that?', 'Adult who?', 'Maybe a young adult...', 'Was your question meant for me?', 'Oh, shit, I guess I am one.' Having sex, buying a house or having children were a few of the other answers I got. I guess that's when true responsibility hits. *Ah, that word again.* You know, the Don't Get Pregnant, Pay Your Mortgage, Keep the Kid Alive. Fun stuff. My essential chocolate shop to alleviate my cranky mood seems irrelevant in that context, doesn't it?

Regardless of who you ask, we all have different, yet valid moments when we feel somewhat adult. There are no wrong answers.

For me, it was seeing the number 30 on a birthday cake that did it. That was the moment. I wasn't expecting it. It really had not occurred to me until that number was staring me right in the face. *The fact that I don't recognise anyone singing on the radio anymore, apart from when it's Smooth FM, should've been a warning too, let's be honest.* Not even the yummy Victorian sponge cake underneath that candle could remove the sting I felt to see 30 on there. It stung, not because I wasn't happy or grateful for the life I have, but because it was the wake-up call I secretly needed to shake my life up and shape it with fulfilling choices. So, yeah, my immediate and only thought that day was: 'Boy, I really do need to get my shit together.'

Despite fighting it for most of my twenties, I think it's safe to say, from the stories I'm about to tell you, that I'm officially an adult now. I've always been late to the party but I made it here eventually.

Turning 30 feels different for everyone obviously. Some look forward to it, some dread it, some do not remotely care either way. Thirty does feel different for me somehow. It feels good, I think... Dare I say it, but there's a sense of relief. It's a fresh new decade. Aside from the momentary dig at that 30 candle, I realised it really is just a number. I know that's what people always say but it's true. It's not even about the number, it's about the life lessons. And how you choose to implement them in a new decade. Looking back on the last 10 years, I realise there have been *many* lessons. Which is why I would like to take this opportunity to sit you all down, including myself, and *listen* to what I have to say. Because in the middle of the messy, scary, impossible, frustrating, disappointing moments I went through, and that we ALL go through, there have been wonderful, glorious, joyful, stunning ones too.

My thirtieth birthday involved spending a great deal of the day sitting on the living room floor in my West London flat, surrounded by beautiful gifts, cake and champagne, reminiscing about the absurdity and hilarity that defined my twenties. I'm not here to complain. However, I can examine the journey. It's definitely been a ride so far. A beautiful, messy ride, one that I'm about to share, in the hope that I, *and perhaps you,* can find comfort, inspiration, laughter and even serenity in the fact that we are all supposed to learn, keep learning, allow ourselves to be imperfect and strive to be better.

I will not be holding back here. We'll be going through it all: the relationship with the body, the evil that is anxiety, figuring out how to trust our instincts, my more than unusual work life as an actor, and how work isn't meant to define us. We'll dig into my disastrous love life, *you're in for a treat,* how our friends and family shape us more than we think, and finally how it is possible to find our identity, and stay true to it, in this limitless, daunting world. A hell of a lot to unpack there, I'd say. All these chapters work independently of each other, meaning you can feel free to dip in and out of this book, picking and choosing which chapters you want to read according to your mood. There are no rules!

Oh, one last thing. I want to preface this by saying that I am by no means an expert on life. I have no clue what I'm doing or what's going on most of the time. The tips from my infamous Aunty Ange alter-ego listed at the end of every chapter, are simply useful things that worked for me. *Again, I'm not an expert here!* But the lessons and situations I've been in, from puberty to the age of 30, have been very real, *very* eclectic, and have taught me far more than I imagined at the time. Everything you will read in this book is 100 percent true: the good, the hilarious and the downright bad. It all happened. *Yes, even that dating story.* Laugh away, cry away, drink away my friends! Do with it as you please. I can only hope you benefit from these stories and relate to them as much as I have learned from them.

Now, let's get started.

I. BEING KIND TO
YOUR BODY

Be kind to your body. This is a big one. I'm starting with this because I did *not* grant that kindness to my body in my early twenties. Not by a long shot. Loving and accepting your body is a process. It's taken me years, and I'm still not completely there yet. It's certainly not a consistent feeling. There are great days and not-so-great days. But there is progress for sure. And that's huge. However, this appreciation for my body was not a sudden magical change of mindset. It has certainly felt impossible at times to show any sort of kindness towards my body. The relentless judgement I directed at it was intense. Harsh moments were lived, but I have somehow come out the other side, with a brighter and more appreciative outlook. Which means you can too. Whatever your relationship is with your body now, I promise you, being kind to it is the only requirement. Now, let's figure out what Being Kind To Your Body actually means.

What I'm going to talk about in this chapter is my personal journey with my body – what I found out in the process, how my mindset shifted, how my respect for what the body can overcome massively increased, how what we feel is not an isolated case, how the idea of perfection is a myth that is detrimental to everyone and how, ultimately, accepting our bodies and the uniqueness of our bodies is one of the most important things we can do for our own fulfilment.

Granted, it's one of the most serious chapters in this book, but a vital one. Let's dive in!

Living With My Body

From the ages of 10 to 19, I grew up in France, in beautiful Brittany. My mother is French and most of the French side of my family are women. Mostly because my grandmother had only girls, therefore the presence of women was more dominant from an early age... *along with divorces, break-ups, and single mums taking over.* One thing you might say about French women is that they are known to be thin. I try not to generalise, but studies have shown that French women are amongst the most petite frames in Europe. And my family was no exception. My mum, my aunts, my cousins – all of them are petite, thin women. Without really trying and most of the time with bread and cheese in their mouths. *Annoying, I know.*

I, on the other hand, discovered that, when my teenage years – and the curves that come with them – arrived, I was simply not built the same. I didn't really think much of this until puberty hit when I was 14 years old and I gained some weight. Nothing unusual or abnormal about that, and I didn't gain a huge amount of weight, but when all I had to compare myself to were my size zero French relatives, it stung. It was really upsetting to me. Why was I suddenly a size 10 when my cousins were super skinny? I remember coming home from school when I was 16, crying in pain because I had spent the entire day squeezed into my cousin's jeans that were clearly too small for me. And that's when the idea that my body wasn't looking how I wanted it to be, really began. I became obsessed with looking like my cousin. It didn't occur to me that my body was different and that there was, in fact, nothing wrong with that. Instead, I thought, 'OK, how can I lose weight fast? How can I be thin like her?' while my body was obviously still developing as a woman.

Puberty is a really weird time for everyone. No one really warns you about anything. It just happens. I can only speak for girls here – I'm sure guys go through some stuff as well – but the second you get your first period, there is a change. We become so wary of everything. And insecure. Either you get boobs really early, or you don't get them at all and you worry. You get acne, you gain weight, and your hormones are all over the place. It's uncontrollable. And confusing. I had zero control over what my body was doing. It's not like I was suddenly eating way more, yet my jeans didn't fit anymore and that's all I could think about for a while. And when you have skinny relatives trying to comfort you, it just doesn't work. It made me wish I was more like them. It seemed to me that being skinny would make you happier.

So, how could I achieve this and 'be happier'? *The upsetting reality of what goes through teenagers' and women's minds, mine included*. Well, it started with the belief that starving myself and not eating proper meals would make me thin. Which meant trying every stupid diet under the sun. Remember that Special K diet? What on earth was that about? A 30g bowl of cereal for dinner? Yes please, sounds amazing. Eating *just* soup seemed to work for a bit until I fainted in school. And here's the thing: losing weight when you're still growing is close to impossible and really not recommended for your health. For me, we were talking a few kilos that were *normal* for a

16-year-old. But I was just not having it. I was going to be hungry and lose whatever weight I could. Unsurprisingly, it didn't work. When I look back on those couple of years, I feel a little sad for that teenage girl who was frustrated and didn't feel like she was good enough because she wasn't stick thin. I was never overweight, not even close, but the pressure I put on myself to look a certain way was relentless. My stubborn brain had decided what I had to look like without asking my body's permission.

I have strong memories of crying on my mum's shoulder because I had weighed myself, again, and hadn't lost that extra kilo. All that suffering, when what I should've done is let my body just adapt to growing as a normal teenage body should. The endless magazines parading actresses and models who didn't eat wasn't helpful either. I grew up with the Olsen twins, Lindsay Lohan, Hilary Duff, Jennifer Aniston and Britney Spears, women who were looked up to as ideals of physical perfection. They were used as body references. Obviously, now that I look back, most of those girls had eating disorders at some point and they were far from being ideal role models for young girls. *Aside from Jen of course, what a gem*. What I saw in glossy magazines was the image I had of beauty. And that was before social media... Nowadays, on top of whatever we might be going through and feeling about our bodies, the presence online of supermodels and influencers, with unrealistic, and often highly filtered, faces and bodies is relentless, unrealistic, harmful, and simply not reflective of real bodies. Images of this unattainable idea of perfection are displayed everywhere. We are surrounded by them. Undoubtedly, it can be a tough mindset to break out of.

Luckily, the stupid diet phase didn't last. I think my friends, my boyfriend at the time and simply having fun as a teenager took over my inclination to be harsh on my body. Or maybe just being exhausted with it all overcame that obsession for a while. For a minute, it looked like I was moving into acceptance... Or so I thought.

When I moved to London at 19, I was so focused on acting and getting my career started that not much else mattered. It was also the first time I was living on my own and in charge of my own life. It was scary, exciting, confusing and hard. I didn't have a lot of money and I was working as a waitress while also auditioning. I was so consumed by work that I simply was not eating enough. Looking back on it now, I honestly don't know how I thought that way of living was remotely sustainable. Living off cans of corn and beans on toast...not ideal. I lost so much weight so quickly that I didn't have my period for four months. As a woman with hypochondriac tendencies, I have no idea why I didn't harass my GP about it. I guess when you're so caught up in life, you don't see the major warning signs right in front of you. It took someone else to make me see them clearly.

After a year in London, I went home to France to see my friends and family. I distinctly remember the looks on their faces when they saw me after such a long time. My best friend pulled me aside and said I looked like a ghost of myself. And she was right. I was pale and my eyes were huge, my hair was thinning, my cheeks were gone, as were my thighs. I wore 14-year-old clothing at 19. I actually found a pair of jeans from this time the other day and tried to put them on, but they didn't go past my knees. I was wafer-thin. Listening to her concerns helped me quickly get back on my feet and I began to learn how to take care of myself. I have a few photos of that week back home and I honestly can't believe I didn't realise how much weight I'd lost. I had reached the point of being so underweight that the doctor had to put me on the pill to make my period come back. It's baffling how we can just go through life, thinking we're doing OK, taking care of ourselves, to then realise it wasn't OK. It was survival. It was harmful and damaging. I was very lucky to have good people around to wake me up from that way of living.

The thing about that phase was that I wasn't consciously *not* eating. My circumstances were a major part of my weight loss. For the first six months in London, I was living in a house with seven people. It was gross and unsettling, and cooking meals in the kitchen didn't really appeal to me. I was always running around the city between castings and work and maybe avoiding that house as much as possible. There was no routine and no time to rest. That's what I thought life in London as an actress was supposed to be. I'm not making excuses, what I am saying is that sometimes you can get caught up in bad habits and it takes someone from the outside to shake you out of them. And thankfully, I was ready to listen when they did.

Luckily, I eventually started earning more money and got myself out of that horror house. I was in a more settled place, living with two lovely girls, and acting in some great productions. I had gained some pounds and was at a much healthier weight. What happened next took me by surprise, though. An unpleasant surprise. I thought I had overcome the 16-year-old body image issues at that point but they resurfaced when I least expected them. My career was taking off and I felt a bit more stable. Yet somehow, without really any reason, my stress levels were through the roof. I could not shake it off.

I'm a worrier and I didn't know any tools, back then, on how to deal with the constant flow of potential disaster scenarios I was making up in my head. 'What if this casting director thinks I'm too fat for this role? What if I spill coffee on the main actor on set? Am I going to get fired from this movie because I'm simply not good enough? Maybe they've made a terrible mistake in casting me?' Now, everyone has different ways of dealing with food when stress and anxiety appear. Some people don't eat at all when they are stressed. I do the opposite. I eat whatever I can find. I'm also someone who likes to control things. Combining these two things led to this: every time I felt stressed, anxious and like I was losing control of my emotions, I would grab anything that was in my cupboard, eat the whole thing and then I would make myself throw up. To me, it seemed like a good way to make myself feel better for a moment and then purge so I wasn't gaining any weight. That way, I felt like I was controlling my food intake and also levelling out my stress. I was killing two birds with one stone: my anxiety and maintaining my goal weight. *What a fucking awful solution, right?* On top of that, it became something I knew I could control when everything in my life was unstable and uncertain. *The life of an actor ain't no picnic.*

This phase didn't last, thankfully. I knew what I was doing was hurting me and, eventually, I knew I was the only one who could put a stop to it. That said, it did take a specific painful moment for this to happen.

One day, I was in the bathroom, throwing up the packet of biscuits I had scoffed down, when suddenly I realised I had cut the back of my throat with my nail. I was terrified. Seeing blood on my finger really hit me. How could I possibly be inflicting this kind of pain and damage on myself? And what was it doing to my insides? I felt stupid and ashamed. I was hurting myself all on my own – and for what, exactly? I was a healthy weight and surely this wasn't helping my stress levels in any way. This madness had become more of a habit. It had to stop. And it did, that day. None of it was worth living that moment again. I wrote it down in my diary that day and never looked back. I was choosing health. It was going to be the finish line for that chapter of my life.

Now, there is no way you can expect to suddenly feel better about it all. It's a process. I can't say I was never tempted to run to the bathroom after eating too much of something, but I can honestly say that I never did it again. I learned to stop being so hard on myself, to know that eating that extra piece of cake was not going to destroy me and that forcing myself to throw up would only make me feel worse. I weighed the pros and cons every time that temptation came until it slowly disappeared from my mind. Today, I wouldn't even think of putting myself through that again and you can *bet* I am going to eat that extra piece of cake. I have learned to love my body the way it is. Sure, some days I'm not a fan, but I don't let hate or judgement come in anymore. My body is curvier and, in my opinion, more beautiful today than it was when I was a size four. I'm not starving myself and I'm not binge eating. I'm eating what I want, in moderation. And my body and brain have settled on a weight and figure that suits us both.

It doesn't mean the work ends there, though. If you're anything like me and have gone through something similar, or are still in it, you'll know that there are steps to all of this.

The first one, as I've discussed, is ending the self-harming behaviour. If you don't think you can, ask for help. Talk to someone – anyone, frankly. Talking about it makes it real, which means you must take action and really work on treating yourself better. Baby steps, but any step forward counts.

Then, we have what was a big step for me: forgiving myself for what I put myself through. At first, I never wanted to think about those dark moments. I was ashamed and angry and didn't want to revisit any memories of them. To be honest, I don't think about those years often now, but I still like to observe how much I've grown from time to time, which helps in dialling down on the shame I once felt. I have to remind myself that I have learned from those mistakes and that they don't make me weak. Far from it. They made me stronger. I rose above it all. I overcame something huge and chose to treat myself better and with the respect I deserve. I chose to be *kind* to myself. And I think that's pretty amazing!

Once you've forgiven yourself, the next and final step is accepting that you will live with the scars, mentally and physically.

Mentally, I've come to a point where I am at peace with that chapter of my life. I can't take any of it back. I know I have those memories and I can't really forget them, but I also know that I won't go back to that place. I've learned my lesson; I've recovered and moved on. Those memories can sit here quietly and observe what happens next.

Physically, I have many noticeable stretch marks on my thighs because of the amount of weight I lost very suddenly back then. I will have those stretch marks forever. I used to hate them, avoiding shorts and skirts for so long; I was convinced that's all people saw. I hated them because they were also a reminder of what I had done to myself. I wanted them gone and forgotten. I spent a fortune on creams. *Oh, and if I can tell you anything, it would be that those creams DO NOT WORK. Your scars may fade a little, but they won't disappear.* After some time – and endless brands of useless creams – I decided that those stretch marks were there to remind me that my body is strong. I've overcome some dark shit, but I've also healed. Scars mean strength and resilience. They tell your story. They mean something. They are beautiful. And so are you.

I am deeply grateful and proud when I look back at the journey I've had with my body. Proud because, when I was mistreating my body, I never thought I'd be accepting of it. I look back at my twenties now and can see how far I've come and how those harsh phases, which felt never-ending, were meant to be experienced for me to appreciate my body now. I hope you can look back, now or some day when you're ready, and hopefully realise that you've come further than you thought, by just accepting yourself. And if that doesn't seem achievable yet, then let me try and convince you otherwise.

Your Body Is a Miracle

Everyone is different and has a unique experience with their body. Some are completely comfortable with how their body looks, and that's wonderful. But most of us will go through some self-critical moments – moments that can last years, sometimes decades – mostly because we don't fully acknowledge the beauty of our bodies and what they actually do for us every day. We're too busy focusing on what's wobbly, what's not 'perfect'. *I hate that word.* We ask ourselves why our bodies keep changing and why won't they stop; why don't we look like that particular person or why does this part of my body not look how I want it to. It's endless and if you let it, it can go on forever. But have you ever stopped to think about how amazing our bodies are and what they can overcome?

I'll give you a small example of how my thought process changed in relation to how I viewed my body. When I turned 26, I decided to join the gym for the first time in my life. *Don't give me that look. I know, OK. Super late to the gym extravaganza.* At 26, I was starting to come to terms with how my body looked and I was not mad at it. I had overcome the eating disorder and was on a healthy track. However, aside from eating well, I did want to gain some muscle. So, I went to my GP for advice. *I should remind you that I am a major hypochondriac, so my GP will probably feature a lot in this book*

– just go with it. He suggested I try the gym and do some weight training. I didn't think I was going to get anywhere with it, really, and so without much conviction, I got myself to the gym and really made it a point of going three or four times a week for a month. *Ok, ok, there may or may not have been a really cute fitness instructor hanging around who, unknowingly, helped me keep going to the gym.*

To my surprise, after a month, I was actually noticing progress. I was feeling my muscles grow, muscles I didn't even know I had. But, more importantly, I was feeling stronger every week that went by. And I have to say, that was empowering. The goal was never to look perfect, but to feel healthier and stronger. And it worked! I looked in the mirror after that month of training, seeing the progress in front of my eyes, and that's when I realised something pretty basic, but hugely important: What our body does every day is kind of a miracle.

Think about it. Your body has been there for you since you were born. It's been supporting you even when you weren't ready to support it back. It has done *so* much for you. It's carried you this far, forgiven you for all the mean things you ever said about it and continued to be here for you even after you've abused, ignored, mistreated and grimaced at it in the mirror time and time again. It's evolved with you. I went from being an insecure, chubby teenager, to a skinny twig, to a healthier, stronger woman with actual abs and muscles. I had so much more appreciation for what my body could endure and also what it could make me do. It's just been there, every step of the way.

Our body takes us places every single day. It carries us through the best and the worst days. It is stronger than you give it credit for. You only have to turn on the news or look online to find the most incredible stories of what people have physically overcome. People who have been told they would never walk again, do. Burn victims heal. Life-changing accidents happen and are overcome. Many beat the most aggressive of cancers, and the darkest depths of eating disorders. Our bodies survive childbirth, for crying out loud! That kind of pain seems insurmountable and yet, the body still walks, still runs. It's our best ally. Your body will fight with you; it is on your side. It is yours and yours only. You only have one, so why not love it and take care of it, like it's been taking care of you since day one?

Instead of resenting the stretch marks, the imperfections, the cellulite, the extra pound you've gained over Christmas, or whatever it was you were fixating on that day, remind yourself that your body is strong and, most of all, one of a kind. No one else has the same one. It's your own unique vessel. Your body is a freakin' miracle. It is *meant* to be different and unique. Don't try to make it look like something you think is more beautiful when you already have a body that is entirely one of a kind. Love it and embrace it completely.

So, every time you look at your whole body in the mirror and start judging it or cringing at it, stop yourself. Finding things to criticise in that mirror is too easy. It's a cop-out. It comes naturally, right? Sure. But what exactly do you think I mean when I say, 'Be KIND to your body?' It means rising above that criticism. THANK your body – out loud if you have to. Thank it for all that it does for you, 24/7.

Look at your body, top to bottom, and remind yourself what it does for you every day. Think of all the things you can do with it! Consider how it lets you express yourself in so many amazing ways. For me, the realisation came with something as mundane as going to the gym and becoming stronger. But I could also say that my body gives me the opportunity to act, to express myself on stage and on screen. What a gift! The list is endless of what our bodies offer us. From dancing to swimming in the ocean, travelling all around the world to horseback riding, yoga, combat training – anything! That's the beauty of your body. It's there for you, always. Isn't that amazing? All you have to do is keep it healthy and treat it with affection. That's your only job.

Admittedly, it took me a while to get to a place of even being able to look at my entire body and be grateful, but I think I got there. What's the alternative? Hating it? What's the bloody point of that? That won't bring me joy, happiness or peace. It'll just put me in a bad mood, which will piss everyone off, spread negativity and lead to nothing good. It's simply exhausting. And I'm 30 now. I don't have time to waste cringing at my body. And neither do you.

So, learn to love your body. For all that it does to support you, it deserves it. Please. It's an important one.

You Are Not Alone in This

One thing I wish I had known more about when I was going through those tough times, is the number of people who were going through exactly the same thing, every single day. In the middle of it, in my early twenties, I vividly remember feeling quite isolated and lost, feeling like there was no one else to confide in, no one who could understand. It was just not discussed, a decade ago. What I didn't know is that talking to someone about what I was dealing with was also going to make it real. And then maybe the problem would have to be solved. I guess I wasn't ready for that. Keeping it all inside is not the answer, though. It makes us spiral out of control and into darkness.

I was convinced I was alone in that situation and that no one would understand. Or even worse, they'd judge me for what I was doing and feel sorry for me. So, staying silent felt like a better alternative than dealing with people's opinions and looks. Well, I was wrong. A few years after I recovered from that eating disorder, I was out with one of my best friends and somehow we got to talking about eating habits and acid reflux. She told me she had quite a lot of issues with reflux since she used to have an eating disorder a few years ago. I couldn't believe it. It was around the same time I was dealing with the same issue and we had never talked about it before. I also would never have known, my friend being the slender gal that she is and the most outgoing, confident person ever. I would never have known that she was going through what I was going through.

It made me both sad that we hadn't shared this sooner but also reassured me that my experience was not an isolated case. Not only was I not alone, but talking about it massively helped me forgive myself and move on from it. I also now know that if I ever need some guidance or need to talk about my past experiences, I have that person who will get it. It was also a huge lesson in discovering that we really do not know what is going on in someone else's life. They can seem like the happiest person ever but might be dealing with something far darker underneath.

And I can't stress it enough, if you are going through something similar or anything that is harmful and hurting you, please reach out to someone. I promise you it can only help. Don't keep all those feelings in. Find someone to talk to. You'll probably be surprised to discover that you're not alone in having these emotions. Everyone has their own demons and sharing our struggles helps us push through them.

Speaking of other people, here is something else I learned in my twenties: no one actually cares or even notices that extra pound around your belly. Or that random spot on your face, or anything else you thought was a big deal at the time. Those tiny things you might call flaws are not worth the time or energy you spend fixating on them. Finding stuff wrong in the mirror is wasted energy. I promise you, no one will care about that scar or that mole. Those things make you unique and beautiful.

I used to have serious insecurities about my hair. My hair is straight, fine and I don't have a lot of it. It's nothing special but it's also not terrible. However, when you have such insecurity about something very visual that you see every day, it's very easy to become obsessed with making it 'better'. Not only did I spend a fortune on vitamins, doctor's appointments and products that promised me voluptuous, shiny, insane hair, *that I never got*, but I also went through a phase of comparing my hair to the hair of every other girl I encountered. I became so frustrated, angry and sad about this because I couldn't see past the hair! One day, I met up with my best friend in a cafe and I was feeling so insecure about my hair that my whole mood was affected. I was genuinely sad. She asked me what was wrong, and I broke down crying, explaining that my thoughts for the past few months had been consumed with how crappy my hair was and that I couldn't change anything about it. She was very surprised. She took my hands in hers and calmly said: 'Your hair is beautiful. Do you know how much I want that natural colour of yours and wish that my hair was straight!' My best friend has gorgeous, voluptuous, curly, thick hair. I just couldn't understand how she didn't fangirl over her own hair and was even remotely thinking about my hair colour.

Turns out, I had become obsessed with something that no one even noticed or had given any thought to. I hadn't even considered all the other things I actually *love* about my face and body. I had created an insecurity and made it bigger in my head, and even worse, I had thought everyone else was cringing at my own head. If you ask me now, *and if I'm being brutally honest about myself here,* this is pretty much what self-centred looks like. It's quite egocentric to assume people are going to be fixating on the one thing you're insecure about when it's 100 percent more likely that they are focusing on their own insecurities. All that worrying is wasted energy and it's negating all the other beautiful things you were gifted with.

Embracing and accepting everything that you are is literally the only thing you have to do. As long as your body is healthy and doing its job, let it be. And remember, every single person, even the most beautiful person you can encounter, will have some insecurity about themselves.

Be kind to yourself and learn to accept who you are – the whole package.

Paying Attention To Your Body

The whole point of this chapter is to remind everyone to be kind to our bodies. It's something we can definitely lose sight of. Life gets in the way. We work too much, eat crappy food, don't sleep as much as we should, etc. If you do all of that for too long, I can guarantee you your body will not sit back, watch and do nothing. It will poke back and send you some important signals. Maybe you should slow down, rest, maybe don't eat that greasy take-out food for the fourth day in a row, and maybe stop looking at your phone before bed because you know you won't sleep well.

Being kind to your body also means listening to it when it feels strained.

When it needs a rest.

I'm a Londoner so I'm naturally drawn to a fast-paced life and I can get really comfortable in that insane, chaotic lifestyle. I'm sure a lot of city people around the world would agree. But eventually, you will crash. Your body won't accept it any longer. And you can bet that it will make itself heard somehow. 'Burn out' is a very common thing and it certainly happened to me. When I went back home to France after those months of working non-stop, travelling, partying, not eating proper meals and not taking care of myself in London, I completely crashed. On top of dealing with unhealthy eating habits and my friend's reaction to my state, my body shut down with exhaustion. That was its way of telling me to CHILL OUT.

Paying attention to where your emotions and tensions sit in your body is equally important. And I'm not talking about the cracking knees! *Although I really think I'm too young to have every bloody limb crack like that.* Tiredness, heartache, sadness, frustration. Those emotions sit deep in your body. They hide, and if not dealt with properly, they manifest themselves abruptly (see the chapter Anxiety and Stress for a solid example). You have to learn how to deal with your emotions upfront, although that took me some time, for sure.

As an actor, I get rejected pretty much on a weekly basis, and I became an expert in shoving down feelings or simply brushing them off. This can work for a while but eventually, everything pops up and, once again, your body is usually the one to let you know.

For instance, I was given a Thai massage a few months ago by my aunt. I had never heard of this type of massage before and admittedly hadn't done any research on it before going in. *I kind of wish I had because I was expecting a calm, soft and chill hour with some nice music and relaxed muscles at the end. Nope.* Beforehand, my aunt told me a Thai massage is for people with anxiety, depression and aches and pains – exactly what I needed, I thought.

Anyway, she laid me down on this huge mattress and, from the soles of my feet to the top of my head, she found every single pressure point possible and applied as much pressure as she could until she felt the muscle had relaxed into its natural healing state. As she was going through my whole body, she explained to me what every part meant. Our right thigh is where we hold the heaviness of our love life and the relationships we've had. *That side was tense for sure.* The left side is all the weight of our work life and ambitions. *Also quite sore.* She massaged until the muscle was released. I could go on and on about all the points she found that were sore. I will spare you.

The one part I did find really interesting was when she came to applying pressure under my right ribs, where my liver and diaphragm are, and could not get in. It was blocked. She asked me when was the last time that I had yelled or expressed anger out loud. I thought for a moment...I literally could not remember. I'm not someone who gets angry and shouts, I usually just kill someone with a deadly look, which does the trick. As homework, my aunt told me to go home and scream – punch something, release any potential, undealt-with anger that I was clearly hanging on to. She did manage to relax that part of my body after a few attempts but it didn't stop me from going home, taking a pillow and yelling into it at the top of my lungs. And boy, did it feel good.

My point is that we are not always aware of what we keep bottled up inside, but our body certainly is, and it lives with those tensions until it becomes too much for it to handle.

So, deal with your shit. Where do things hurt? Heartbreak, shame, joy, anger, stress. Where do they live inside you? What do they do to your body? Deal with all of it head-on; observe your emotions and how you deal with them. Everyone, especially you and your body, will be much happier if you do. Body and mind work hand in hand. Much more is accomplished if they are synced together.

And get to know your body. Keep learning and be curious about it. Inside and out. The more you know, the more confident and comfortable you will be with it. And most importantly, make sure that anyone who tries to enter that space respects it as much as you do (more on that later in the Love chapter).

The good news is the people who told me that the older you get, the more confident you feel, well, those people were correct. It's the truth. You simply won't want to waste time wishing your body was different or wishing it conformed to what the world deemed 'perfect' at the time. Fuck that. You have what you have, embrace it.

If you're anything like me, you'll simply go, 'Ah fuck it, I'll have that second piece of cake and won't fit in those jeans for a week and I'll be happier for it.' I'm not saying be like me, *I swear too much and I really do have a chocolate addiction issue*. But I am saying, please try and give less of a shit about being 'perfect'. Be YOU. The freedom and relief you'll feel will be worth it.

So go! Go explore and uncover what your body has to offer. And, if there is one thing to remember from this chapter, it is that your body is your home and your only job is to be attentive and kind to it. Give it the respect it deserves. It'll return the favour.

AUNTY ANGE TIPS

Everyone is different when it comes to making themselves feel better in their own skin. Here are a few things I do to practice self-care and self-love:

- Scream into a pillow. Doctor recommended, guys.

- Work out. I don't necessarily mean the gym. In fact, apart from the cute fitness dude, I'm not really a fan of the gym. I do like classes, though, and because I get bored quickly, I like doing a mix of things. Pilates, yoga, swimming, ultimate frisbee... Yes, you heard me. Whatever floats your boat. And if you don't have the money right now to go to classes, there are SO many free classes on YouTube that are really diverse and suitable for any level you're at. It's all about listening to your body. If you think your body needs a boost, push yourself to get it moving. It helps, I promise.

- Have a deeply relaxing bath. Preferably with a glass of wine and some George Michael.

- Try a face mask. I feel a lot better when I've done a face mask, have moisturised whatever needs to be moisturised and gone make-up-free for a few days. It gives my skin time to breathe and I feel like I've treated it well.

- Write notes to yourself. My mum writes Post-it notes and sticks them on her bathroom mirror: positive, empowering affirmations to remind herself that she's beautiful and strong. How wonderful is that!

- Notice what you like about your body. If your insecurities are becoming a little too loud, try to spend a few minutes every day writing down what you actually like about your body.

- Go for a walk. Don't diss it 'till you try it. In 2020 and 2021, those walks saved us, didn't they? They do help the mind. Bring your music with you. Or a podcast!

These tips may seem simple, but they do help lift my spirits. If you have your own tricks, don't wait until you feel really down to use them. Do them weekly; get into those good habits. Get your butt movin'. Politely and respectfully, she says.

II. IDENTITY: WHO YOU ARE AND WHO YOU ARE NOT

I will bet you right now that every single person at some point or another will ask themselves the inevitable question: Who am I?

It's an important question. It's a valid question. It's a big question. And here's the thing. There will, without a doubt, be times when we're really not sure what the answer to that question is. Or the answer might change over time. Regardless, it's not a nice feeling, waking up one day, wondering who the hell this person is, lying in bed, living this life. And since no one you know seems to be having that conversation, it makes you think, 'Oh no, am I supposed to know exactly who I am? Why am I not sure? What does that mean? Why do I not know who I am? What's changed?'

My twenties, for me, were full of those moments. And I didn't realise that this was normal for a really long time. Turns out, if I had paid close attention and spoken out about my own doubts, I would've noticed many people going through the same thing.

Figuring out who you are is not an easy path. What *is* easy is completely losing track of who you are, who you might be trying to be or who you're trying to emulate. You think you've found yourself one minute and the next you have no clue where that person's gone or if you even like the person who is looking right back at you in the mirror. I've had my fair share of freak-out moments when it comes to my identity, but having passed the thirty mark now, I can proudly say that I've come a long way from the endless questioning, worrying and doubt that I once put myself through. I might not have all the answers about who I am today but I definitely have come a long way from the many crying on the floor moments, wondering who the hell I was meant to be and why everything was so difficult. *Dramatic guys, remember I'm dramatic.*

In my twenties, there definitely were a few steps I had to take in order to figure out how to be aligned with myself and become my own person. But it's tricky. How is anyone meant to figure out who they are? And if you lose yourself, why does that happen and where does that lost person go? Am I allowed to change and what does that mean? Why do I care what other people think? If everyone is going down that one route, does this mean I should? And why don't I want to do what everyone else is doing? The questions are endless, but they are also very important for self-awareness and growth. We will go through all the messy stages and, hopefully, by the end of this chapter, you'll have realised, just as I did, that who you are without all the noise around you, as a unique individual, is enough.

Asking Yourself the Right Questions

Life can be really fast-paced. Every day, we juggle a million different things and don't really have time to stop and take everything in. We get up, we work, we buy food, cook the food, do laundry, see friends, try to maintain a relationship, go on dates, go through break-ups, move in and out of places, get a dog, hopefully, book a holiday. There are marriages, events, birthdays, baby showers, housewarming parties, business meetings, job interviews, and the list goes on and on. I don't even have kids yet and I still struggle to balance it all out.

My point is that we go through life packing in as much as we can, at an alarming rate. So much so that, in the midst of it all, we can go years without really asking ourselves some important questions. I believe the two most important ones, in all areas of our life, and which we can so often overlook, are: Who am I? and What do I want?

The answers to these questions can change over time, of course. But they need to be asked fairly regularly to keep yourself in check. And I'll tell you now, I did NOT do this, which meant I lost track of those two things more often than I ever expected to.

It's really interesting because, as teenagers, we go through some monumental changes. We step into the path of becoming an adult. We become an actual person. We develop opinions and personalities. We grow, mentally and physically, and at the time, we think that who we are then is it. It's the finish line. This is who we are now, at 19 or 20 years old. This is who we're meant to be.

Sure, we definitely cover the basics in our teens. Our personalities and character traits are pretty much established. We've made some decisions already on who we want to be or at least how we want to be perceived, and we have some sort of idea of what we want out of life. But that is not the end.

Who you are as a teenager is just a stepping-stone across the river of what's to come. You've just about scratched the surface on what you want in life and what person you can be. You haven't even begun the process of becoming you yet. You just think you have.

As a 17-year-old, I was quite confident in what I wanted and didn't want. I knew from an early age what I wanted to do for a living. I knew that I liked boys. I knew I didn't really want to stay in my hometown. I was very outgoing, social and independent. I was very true to myself, very much a no-bullshitter...*still am*. But the stakes are lower when you're young. What you mostly want involves parties, friends, a new pair of boots, a nice holiday, a boyfriend or girlfriend, good grades. It is NOT life-changing. *Although it definitely feels like it at the time.* And I think I was lucky in the sense that I did not care what anyone thought. I was just going to be honest, be truthful to myself and see what happened. So, in that sense, I knew who I was at that time and I wasn't mad about who this person was. I embraced her and I really thought who I was and my goals in life were sort of set in stone and that would be that.

What I didn't anticipate was the shift I went through in my twenties. Everything felt tremendously costly. I felt like the stakes were so high that I didn't know what the right decision for me was anymore. I lost perspective because everything felt too big.

Being a young adult is a really tricky stage to navigate. Even if you thought you knew what you wanted, many things can make you doubt yourself and your actions.

For me, I doubted myself so much that I felt completely lost. That confident teenage gal was nowhere to be found. She felt very far away from the 25-year-old standing there. I had no clue what I was doing, where I was going or even what I wanted anymore. Had I picked the wrong career path? Was I meant to live somewhere else? Did I like what my life looked like? And this was at 25. For some reason, I thought I had to have it all figured out right that second. And when I realised I didn't have it close to figured out, I panicked.

What's difficult is to stop and analyse what's happening. As I said, we all live pretty fast-paced lives. And when you live in London, the pace of life is three times faster. I was juggling castings, finding work, doing actual work, going out with friends, seeing my family when I could, and dating, *which as some of you single people might know, feels like a full-time job at times.* This schedule went on for several years, without me really asking myself where this was going and whether this was actually what I wanted.

Now, the moment I realised I had to stop everything for a second and re-align with myself, was on a random Tuesday night, six months into being 25. I was on another tedious, 'it's going nowhere' date and as I was watching him give me his whole life story, I saw myself leaving my body for a minute, and looking at myself from above. I immediately heard:

'What are you actually doing here? You don't like this guy, you don't even want to date anyone right now, so why are you wasting your evening with someone you're never going to see again? What are you trying to prove? Go home, read that book you've been dying to finish and start making a list of things you actually want to do!'

It was so clear. I was so used to packing up my week with things I thought people in their twenties were supposed to do, that I didn't even realise I was doing it. It was a habit. One I had to break. So, I apologised to my date and left the table. When I got home, I could feel a rush of tears building up and I could not understand why. What the hell was going on with me? I lay on my bedroom floor and sobbed. I remember feeling so overwhelmed with not knowing what I was meant to do next. So, I let it all out. I stayed on that floor until I felt all that anguish leave my body. I couldn't tell you how long I lay on the floor. I picked myself back up when it felt right and assessed the situation. And this is what happened in my brain:

'First of all, pull yourself together, woman. Your life is not THAT bad. Yes, it feels shit sometimes, but ultimately life is OK. You are OK. You are breathing and you are in the comfort of your flat in London. You've had a momentary freakout and maybe you simply needed to let out some residual emotions and relieve some stress, or whatever that was. That's done. We can move on. So, how about we just figure out what the hell is going on with you, uh?'

Literally, that's what happened. Sometimes, you just need to give yourself a pep talk. You might feel crazy by doing it, but if you feel it helps, do it. It gave me a tremendous amount of perspective and gave me some time to observe what was happening.

It's simple. I had hit a bit of a wall. I realised I was conflicted between what I wanted and what other people wanted at my age. I was basically comparing myself to what I *thought* people were supposed to enjoy doing in their twenties. And that was dangerous territory because I was then starting to do things I really had no interest in doing but kept telling myself that I was 25, and everyone else seems to think that's what 25-year-olds are meant to be doing.

So, for instance, dating. I was single and had been casually dating people for a few years and assumed that I was supposed to be constantly dating or looking to be with someone. I was supposed to be having a lot of sex because I was 25 and people keep going on and on about how much sex they are having and how fantastic it is. What does it mean if I don't feel like having sex at this very moment? What does it mean if I want to be alone right now? Was I supposed to have fallen deeply in love with someone already? Why hadn't that happened yet? Am I meant to have had all this experience at 25?

Same with going out. Around 25/26, I didn't really like clubbing anymore. I didn't feel like getting hammered and feeling like death the next day. I had got that out of my system at university. So, what did that mean? Was something wrong with me? Wasn't that what I was supposed to be doing in my twenties?

I was doing all these things because I had this idea, this image in my head, that that's what my twenties had to look like. And suddenly, I realised I didn't like most of these things. I was adapting myself to what I *thought* a 25-year-old should be doing, instead of just creating my own image.

I didn't want to spend money on huge nights out. I didn't want to be dating anyone just because I was single. I *wanted* to be single and see what it felt like. I wanted to spend my money on travelling. I wanted to read good books, have fun house parties and work on film sets. I wanted to earn an amount I was happy with, as opposed to what is considered successful money in London. I realised that I had stressed myself out trying to keep up with a lifestyle I didn't even enjoy.

I slowly made peace with the fact that I enjoyed simpler, quieter, comfier things. And guess what? The second I started doing things for myself, as opposed to things I thought I was meant to do, I felt so much lighter and happier. I felt more like myself again and more confident in that because I knew it made me happy, and that was the most important thing. I was done with the guilt of saying no to things people thought I should do. I was taking myself out of the lifestyle I had lost myself in.

Pleasing people, comparing yourself to what everyone else is doing at any given stage of their lives, well, it's exhausting and, of course, it goes against who you are. You're not meant to do exactly like everyone else! You're meant to live your life for YOU. Because if you don't, you end up spiralling, like I did. It's so important to do what is compatible with your nature and not what you're *supposed* to do. What does that even mean? *Supposed to.* Everyone is different. I know people over 40 who love partying in clubs 'til dawn. And some people at 22 who would rather stay in and order pizza. There is no right or wrong here. What *is* wrong is not listening to what you want to do.

For me, I was hearing a lot of 'Oh you're so young, make the most of it! You have all this energy, go party, go nuts, have fun, go wild!' Nope. The idea of an evening in my flat with friends, wine and games was much more appealing to me. Wearing a tight dress and high heels that made me want to die of pain by the end of the night in a club was not the winner for me.

The same applies to your love life. At some point, you see your friends settling down and you start to wonder if you're meant to do the same. 'Why am I enjoying being single right now? Why don't I feel like settling down yet? What's wrong with me?' you ask yourself. NOTHING. You do you. Enough of the over-thinking and the over-worrying about how you're not living up to everyone else's expectations. It doesn't work that way and will not make you happy.

Your job is to ask yourself what you want and what you don't want and live by that. Truthfully. And through that, who you are will come out. You'll feel more empowered and in tune with yourself and that ultimately makes you a happier, fuller person.

I'm not saying asking yourself those questions is easy. No way. Sometimes it's very difficult to figure out what you like and what you really want because a lot can cloud your judgement and damage who you are. Maybe you're living with negative people, maybe your family is pressuring you in some way, maybe your partner has an influence on you that is difficult to take a step back from, maybe your finances make you feel stuck, maybe you don't like your job anymore and can't figure a way out of it, maybe you don't love the person you're with anymore but don't want to be alone... SO many situations can seem like insurmountable obstacles on the road. However, no matter how difficult or impossible a situation can feel, settling for it isn't living truthfully. These things make us feel like we should settle for a situation; they trick us into thinking that's what we deserve, but that is not what life is meant to be. Life doesn't and shouldn't work that way. You deserve to strive for what you want. You deserve to be happy. And for that, you need to be in tune with who you are and what you want out of this life. DO NOT SETTLE. You are worth more than that.

You are also very much ALLOWED to change your mind about something, or someone. We are ever-evolving individuals, what do you expect? It does not make you a bad or an indecisive person, it just makes you human. Your job is to notice the changes, pay attention to them and then you can move forward on a path that is more suitable for you. It can feel very scary, though. I get it. But wouldn't you prefer to take a leap of faith and risk it, instead of being stuck in a relationship you despise, a place you are bored with, or a job you can't stand?

How many people do you know hate their job? You just gotta go on the Underground in London at 8 am to see the number of miserable faces there, looking like they are travelling towards their death. Most of us go through school, studying, choosing a career, looking for a job, then working at that job and that's it. But when you think about it, so much can change from when you're studying for exams in high school to when you're prepping for this important meeting at the office. Some of us become entirely different people, and then what do you do? When you realise that you've worked so hard, jumped a lot of hoops to then realise you don't think this career was meant for you? Well, it's simple. You stop, ask yourself what you want and then make that happen. The error would be to keep working in a field that isn't fulfilling you. That's the mistake. The alternative is scary but will be much more rewarding in the long haul because you'll be working in something that feels like you.

Granted, it can take ages to realise you don't like where you're at. We can be so consumed by Plan A, whether it's finding the job you've been studying for or finding the person to have a family with, that we just lose sight of what we actually want. It's pretty common and it can be upsetting because our whole identity can all of a sudden be put into question.

Isn't it crazy, though, to think that we can go years without asking these questions when actually, the answers are the most important, life-changing ones! We can be in denial about our true wishes or, worse, we can feel like settling is the best option because going for that risky dream is too scary or feels too impossible to achieve. Just NO. No, no, no. You HAVE to make yourself a priority when it comes to your identity, your wants and your needs. And, contrary to what some people might say, it's not selfish. Quite the opposite. Asking yourself the right questions is essential in order for you to grow. It'll make you a better person, not only for yourself but for the people around you.

So, pause everything for a moment. Stop for one minute and ask yourself: Do you know who you are? Can you write a description down and are you happy with what you've written? What are the differences between who you were as a teenager and now? How do you think your friends describe you? Do you know what you want? Do you have a slight idea of what that might be? Are you actively pursuing that? If not, why not? Are you making a ton of excuses because you're scared? Are you scared you went down the wrong path and it's too late? *It's NEVER too late.* Have your wants changed? How so? Do you think that getting a raise at work is everything you ever dreamed of? How much money would make you satisfied? How much space does work take in your life? Are you missing out on anything else? What do you like to do? What are your hobbies? Do you feel happy? Do you feel fulfilled? What do you want to do next?

If you can answer all of these, firstly, congrats. I certainly couldn't. I'm still not completely sure what I want 100 percent of the time but I do make it a rule to ask myself that a lot more than I used to.

At the age of 30, *ugh, I still can't believe it happened*, I know who I am right now. I also know that it is still possible to lose track of that sometimes, *my Identity Crisis at 28 years old, mentioned a few pages later, is proof of it.* I just have to check in with myself and see if my choices are still in line with me, and my own happiness. Because that is the goal people! Happiness and fulfilment. Don't you forget that!

Ask yourself those questions or, even better, *create* your own questions. Questions that will make you grow and feel more self-assured. Make it your rule. Allow yourself to be honest and maybe discover some truths about yourself you didn't see coming. And keep asking yourself those questions. We never stop growing and it's your responsibility to stay in line with what feels right with who you are. But for that, you need to know who that person is. Start there. We ALL start there.

Other People Do Not Decide Who You Are

Knowing yourself fully is always going to be a work in progress. I don't think there is an actual endpoint. You just grow as much as you can and hopefully become more aligned with your true self as you go. You're going to have times where you feel lost and unsure about what to do next and other times where you'll be confident and know that this is the right path for you. It's just life.

One thing to really look out for is how people affect you and how they might influence your path and who you are on a daily basis. Regardless of how independent and resilient you might be, both of which I like to think I am, some people might get under your skin once in a while and affect how you feel about yourself, or make you question your choices. Once that happens, it's tempting to listen to those people who seem to outweigh your opinions and choices. It's very easy to forget about your wants and needs and be influenced by your surroundings, what other people are doing and what direction they're taking in life. Be cautious.

There is nothing wrong with taking someone's advice or listening to someone's opinions and concerns. Friends and family can be great advisers and they can certainly guide you through some tough decisions and help you in some challenging moments. But you must know that you are in no way obligated to obey or do what is suggested. Your loved ones are important and valuable but allowing them to influence your life choices isn't something I would support or encourage. You are your own person. You have to follow your own journey and since we are all different and have various goals in life, your path will evidently be different from anyone else's.

You are in charge of yourself, which means *you* decide who you are. This means you're going to need to build some boundaries for yourself, some clear guidelines for your reflection and growth. Building boundaries takes time and experience. It's not something that you're going to magically have figured out. You may only work them out when people attempt to cross them.

When lines are crossed, something inside you will awaken and you'll either choose to defend yourself and stand your ground, or you'll follow that outsider voice, regardless of how you feel deep inside. When this happens, and it will happen, you automatically put your identity and your self-worth at risk because you are going against something that doesn't feel quite right. You are letting other people dictate who you are, by not only listening to them but believing that what they are saying about you is true. If you listen to enough people having opinions about you, you'll start to believe them. And by believing people's opinions about you, you're giving them a superpower they do not deserve. You're giving in to their influence and who you are might be in jeopardy.

For instance, I have been asked more times than I can count if I feel more English or more French. I have both nationalities and grew up in both countries. Now, this is something I just didn't even remotely question when I was a teenager. I always identified as both. I had spent equal amounts of time in both countries. I am fully bilingual with no accent in either language. For me, it's always been that I have two nationalities, two passports, one British parent, the other French. Easy. Except, when I moved to London, this became a regular question. On dates, at house parties, at work events, on set etc. 'Are you French or English then? What do you feel most like?' I never thought it would ever come up in conversation as much as it did.

And then, the film industry got involved. An acting agent mentioned that I should maybe start thinking about 'picking a side.' In order to sell me, or my brand, to the film industry, he felt it would be better to choose one nationality so I wouldn't confuse the casting people. I started to feel pressured. I had always been very proud of where I came from and had always embraced both sides. However, this perpetual noise actually started to make me question if I *should* maybe 'pick a side' – pick a country. Could I even do it? Did I actually feel closer to one or the other? And then I got increasingly aggravated. Why should I have to feel more French or more English in order to fit in? I am both. That's who I am and where I'm from. And even though I felt quite strongly about this, being asked it, more than once, did make me doubt myself. Maybe I should make it easier for people and adapt for them? After a lot of back and forth in my head, I made a firm decision. I was not going to stop being me to simplify people's lives. I was not going to diminish a part of me just because it might confuse people. It's not my job. My job is to be me, completely and proudly myself.

Our identities must never be limited by what other people think or assume. Be who you are, who you want to be, regardless of what people might suggest. Only you are in charge of your own identity and happiness and that means not backing down when that is put to the test. Diminishing yourself is going to be damaging in the long haul and you will be the only one to suffer from it. Who you are is enough, no more, no less, no matter how people around you may feel.

Which brings me to another very important point: Do not make yourself smaller to make other people more comfortable. This is a big one. If you accomplish something, if you are proud, if you are loud, if you are confident, if you are happy, if you are thriving, then let it out! This is your time to shine and this doesn't mean you're taking anything away from other people. ALLOW yourself to shine.

I get upset with my mother sometimes because, in recent years, she has let someone influence her personality in ways I didn't think possible. My mum is a radiant presence, a gem of a human, a big warm light who most people are drawn to as soon as she walks into a room. However, she has this real bitch of a 'friend' who is very much the opposite of this. This woman is bitter, jealous and unhappy, and has made it her life's mission to take it out on my mum. *I have not come face to face with this woman in a while because if I did, no 'high road' would be taken.* This woman has made sure that every time my mum has something great to share, like something she's done in the house, a holiday she's enjoyed, or a lovely night out she's had with friends, this woman squashes it, swings an awful comment at her or tries to outshine it with a better, surely fake, story. Not only that but she's become a bully. If my mum is wearing a nice outfit, she'll make sure to criticise it. If my mum has a new hairdo, same thing. It's maddening. Over the years, my lovely mum has slowly chosen to not share anything anymore because she knows the bitch will come out with something that will make her feel bad. It kills me. How dare this woman have so much power over my mum? How dare she have so much influence over her, so much so that my mum is no longer the social, bubbly human she is usually? Because of a bitter woman, my mum is diminishing herself and shining less brightly. Isn't that INSANE?

Of course, my mum is not the only person this has ever happened to. We have all had a friend, a colleague, a family member who can be manipulative, who can make you feel like you can't be 100 percent yourself because you might outshine them. It's infuriating and really sad. Living life like that is dishonest. You're not being true to yourself and that is not a good feeling. It also means you're letting those people win. You're believing them. Those people have the upper hand, and to me, that's unacceptable.

There is enough light for everyone to shine and if people are unhappy or bitter, let them be. But please don't make yourself smaller for their sake. That's not how it works. Aim for your happiness and your well-being and do not CHANGE for anyone. No one should decide who you're going to be and how much of yourself you should display at any given time. Don't give in to that energy. *Mum did end up telling this woman to shove it...I've never been more proud.*

This is why you HAVE to establish some boundaries for yourself. It's so important to have them. Without boundaries, people can walk all over you, influence you, and lead you down the wrong path. And you can be sure that people *will* test your boundaries. Figuring out where to draw some lines will be vital in order to find yourself and build yourself from the ground up.

I was in the hair and make-up trailer on a job recently and I was speaking to my make-up artist who was telling me about this guy she had been dating, on and off, for about a year. She told me it was very casual and that three months into dating, he had ghosted her. He had basically disappeared which left her feeling very confused and annoyed. It was obviously painful for her and it hit her self-esteem massively for a few weeks. She eventually got over it and said to herself that she was better off and that she would not take him back if he ever popped up again. Well, you can pretty much guess what happened next. He texted her after two months and asked her out again. And yes, she did go out with him again, for another five months, until the same thing happened again. She had broken her own rule. She had given in to his wants and sacrificed a little piece of herself by doing so. It was subtle but it was there. She realised it once he was gone again. She knew she had twisted herself to please him instead of choosing herself and her self-worth. It reminded me of my own past relationship where a similar thing had happened (see Love chapter). I wouldn't go as far as saying it bruised my identity, but it easily could've if I hadn't caught myself in time.

As she was telling me this in the make-up trailer, she asked me, 'When do we actually learn how to raise our standards and take what we deserve, nothing less? When does that kick in?'

It was a brilliant question. And my answer went something along the lines of this:

'I think you probably have to get burned a few times for it to shake something inside of you. And that will raise up some clear boundaries. You'll then learn how to stand up for yourself and stick to your guns, and most importantly, not CHANGE your standards or opinions or way of living your life for anyone, especially someone who doesn't treat you with respect. However, in order to do that you have to show yourself the respect you deserve. You have to respect yourself enough to walk away from a situation that doesn't meet your standards anymore. That takes guts, courage and a certain amount of determination. It's not easy but it will feel so much more empowering once it's done and you'll feel much closer to who you are by doing so.' *Clearly, I was having a very enlightened moment when I told her this. Quite proud, might I add... wish I could be that good at giving myself these pieces of advice sometimes!*

Being true to yourself is making sure you are aware of how it feels when you're more focused on other people's opinions rather than living your life for yourself. Are you aware of why you are doing a certain thing? Are you doing it for yourself or someone else? This awareness can be brought to your attention through everyday actions. Take the time to stop and analyse what YOU want, as opposed to what people want you to do. Are you doing something because you're thinking of what other people might say if you don't? Are you going to this party because X, Y and Z said so, and they'll be mad if you don't go? Are you wearing this outfit instead of the one you prefer because your partner doesn't like that one? Are you going on this date because that's what you think you're meant to do on a Friday night when you're single?

The people who truly love you won't care. Do what you want to do.

The other day I was on the phone with one of my friends who was having a really hard time. She was feeling stuck and really didn't feel like herself anymore. She had been with her boyfriend for over six years and had come to realise that she didn't love him anymore. She told me she felt she was losing pieces of herself and didn't know how to get out of this slump. She wanted to travel. She wanted to find herself again, outside of a relationship. The answer seems simple, right? Well, to her it wasn't. She kept telling me that questions were spiralling in her head about what she should do, and what would happen if she actually could bring herself to leave him.

I asked her what questions she was actually asking herself here because to me, the solution was quite simple. It's not an easy thing to break up with someone, sure. But this is a simple thing. She didn't love him anymore. I asked her what was stopping her.

She replied, 'Well, I'm thinking of how our families will react, my family and his. My mum loves him and his family has really been good to me over the years. And what will happen to him? He is a lovely guy. Also, our jobs are very compatible; it's easy. What will it do to him if I leave?'

I was stunned. I asked her to consider thinking about herself for a minute and NOT how everyone else in the world would react to this break-up.

'This is your life, not theirs.' I said. 'This is your happiness, your decision. Pause for a second. How do you think you'll feel if you break up with him? Right now, if you know you've ripped that Band-Aid off and told him you're leaving.'

She paused for a minute and said: 'Relief.'

'That's your answer,' I said.

It's about shutting all that noise around you. Ultimately when it comes to making decisions for yourself and going for what you want, you need to be able to take that leap and not worry about what people will say or do. Others should not be able to decide for you. You do not want to look back at your life in 10 years' time and realise that all the choices you made or were lured into making, weren't yours, and the life you live now isn't one that fits you. You will feel so much more satisfied and fulfilled when you know that your life and your decisions were yours and yours only. It's about taking charge of your life.

And this works the other way around, too. It is not your job to fix or influence people in any way. I struggled with that for a while. I'm a fixer and I like helping people but, sometimes, I've had to force myself to take a step back and stop trying to fix something that I have no control over. I am not responsible for other people's happiness. I can help and I can contribute as much as I can but ultimately, I just had to learn to let people be. You have to let people make those mistakes, choose that career path, and date that person. You have to let people have their own journey even when you don't understand their choices. And definitely stop judging people because they sin differently from you. Every single person has a unique path and that is just how it's supposed to be. It is not your job to decide for them. Let go and let be. I am sure people do the same for you when you're in the middle of making a mistake and you don't see it at the time. We make mistakes to learn from them later on. You can support a person through a lot, but you can't fix them, you can't change them; that's up to them.

We just all have to allow each other to be our own people. Let's be open to advice and guidance but ultimately, our right to be our own self is number one. No one should be given the power to taint that. And as much as you might sometimes want to influence a person in your life, even if you think it's for their greater good, it is not always your call. If you're anything like me, you may have great empathy for other people and are very deeply considerate of others and maybe feel like it's your duty to sway people in the direction you deem best, influence a decision they are making or manipulate them in some way. You can be there for someone, but you can't change who they are, and if you really love them, you shouldn't want to either.

Let people be and do not let people decide who you are. Only you are in charge and when you look back, in how many years' time, I want you to see a life that you chose and that you feel completely matches your vision, not anyone else's. Keep your vision, your identity and your own path in check.

Identity Crisis

Remember that time your mum dyed her hair black and went through a sort of gothic phase and had a much older married boyfriend, who smoked a lot? Or that time your dad bought an awful shiny red sports car, went partying in strip clubs and drank too much? No, just my parents? OK, cool.

So, it turns out those things are called identity crises, guys. And no one is immune to them. You will, without a doubt, go through some sort of identity crisis in your life. One, if not a few. Think of it as a sort of rite of passage. It's completely normal and you will get over it. But brace yourself, it's going to happen. At any time, to anyone. Usually, you get to see a glimpse of it in your parents before it happens to you. All I can say is that seeing my parents go through it was completely bonkers to witness.

When my parents got divorced, it was like all hell broke loose. I would look at my folks and wonder what the hell was going on in their heads. One minute, they were my responsible, mature, tame parents; very much the picture-perfect marriage. A wonderful family dynamic. The next minute, they were divorced, angry, lost and acting like teenagers. They were no longer the parents I grew up with. The 'perfect' image was shattered. Suddenly, they were flawed people. They were vulnerable and making very 'eclectic' – *who am I to say stupid* – life choices. But I guess that's what happens when there is a sudden change in one's life. Often, identity crises are triggered by a major life event, something completely out of the blue that shakes you to your core and makes you rethink where you're at and who you are.

Regarding my mum, I noticed a significant shift in her when she got divorced. I can't speak for her, but I think it was an overwhelming mix of feelings between freedom, relief, anger, confusion and messiness. A rediscovering of herself. When you're married for 14 years, and you have been so used to being a wife and accustomed to being at home with your kids, divorce is a life-shaker. Not only is it deeply unpleasant to have the family dynamic collapse, but your role in the family changes. In Mum's case, she was no longer a wife and had to start planning the next step. She moved countries, got a job and had to start building a social life again, all in a very different setting. All those circumstances can change you. And they did for a bit. She was trying to find herself again as a single mum, as an independent, brave woman. I also think she wanted to remove herself from her old life as much as possible. Her old life as a suburban housewife was very far away now. She was free of it and wanted to embrace that as much as possible.

So, she started hanging out with younger single people. She wanted to feel sexy. She wanted to flirt and be wanted. She started dating again, spent nights out in clubs and bars, picked up smoking and dyed her hair black to match her dark eyeliner. If I go through our photo albums now, I can tell you exactly when those photos were taken according to what gothic make-up Mum was wearing that decade.

Listen, she is a badass. She is fierce as hell, but you could tell she was going through the motions of experimenting with who she was and who she wanted to be in this new era. As a teenager, observing this was both fascinating and alarming. Wasn't I supposed to be the demanding teenager who went out clubbing and came home at 4 am? It was definitely Freaky-Friday for a minute at our casa. No judgement here – my mum is the coolest chick in town, but it was a remarkable shift from the mum I had known so far, home baking our birthday cakes from scratch and not drinking much. I didn't quite understand what was going on. Later, she told me that she needed to go through that crazy party life to find herself again. She needed to feel young, to appeal to men again, to flirt, to feel alive and free in order to rediscover herself after such a major setback. To this day, she says it was the most fun and liberating time of her life and she regrets none of it.

It makes complete sense. And maybe identity crisis isn't the correct term in this case. Maybe I, the teenager, saw it as a crisis because seeing my mum dancing in the same bar I was hanging out in, with my friends, was not exactly what I would call normal. It was unsettling. But now that I look back, I love how, instead of being miserable after her divorce, she took her life into her own hands and created a whole new way of living that suited her at the time. She reinvented herself. So no, maybe not a crisis. Let's call it an identity *shift*. A time when you need to go through something to find yourself again.

This doesn't mean a 'crisis' won't happen again. I was speaking to my mum recently and she was telling me that she isn't sure what the next step is now. She is reassessing who her friends are, what she likes in her life, and whether she wants a serious relationship. She went on about how she had been revisiting memories of her past relationships and that maybe there had been a pattern in her behaviour she now wanted to change. As I was listening to her, I thought, 'Wow, this kind of questioning really CAN happen at any time in one's life.'

These questions tend to arise when we haven't been paying enough attention to ourselves for a really long time and we feel stuck at that moment. It doesn't mean there isn't a way out, there always is, but it does take some sitting down and rethinking about what can be done to get out of a slump. Except that, most of the time, this re-thinking is never done in a calm and efficient way, is it? I don't think it's entirely possible simply because we are human. We don't always have the greatest of perspectives. We keep going until suddenly nothing seems to be going the right way and none of our actions are making sense to us anymore.

My dad definitely went through the motions of an 'identity crisis' too. His identity was very much driven by what his parents wanted for him: corporate job, house, marriage young, kids young. The whole lot. Suddenly, he realised he wasn't living the life he truly wanted for himself. When he finally stepped out of that life, he thought that would be it – he would have found himself again, but it took a lot of left turns and kicking a serious drinking habit for him to find himself again, which is not an easy thing to do. It's a very admirable thing. Having seen him go through all of that throughout my teens and twenties, I am very proud of the man he is now, very much in tune with who he was meant to be. It doesn't mean it wasn't messy for several years though...*I also know he will sue me if I give up any more information than that, so let's move on.*

So there I was, observing this madness, not really thinking that this would ever happen to me, especially at a young age. Turns out, both of my folks were not isolated cases. Everyone will experience some sort of an identity crisis at some point in their lives.

It's just one of those moments where you have no clue who you are anymore. Zilch. Nada. We change so much in one lifetime, it's to be expected really. Except no one warns you of the when, the how and the why. An identity crisis just happens.

Maybe you stopped thinking of yourself as a priority for a while or maybe you changed and didn't realise it. It can all be a bit fuzzy. There are going to be times when you will lose yourself, without any help from anyone but yourself. It's true. We can be our own worst enemy; we can sabotage ourselves all on our own. And when we are lost, we usually try to find ourselves again by doing stupid shit that makes zero sense. And that's something I personally didn't see coming until it actually happened.

My identity *shift* landed a couple of years ago. I woke up one morning and couldn't really understand any of the choices I'd made in my life. I had been hanging out with a group of very rich socialites in Kensington for a few months. I had met them in a club and they had included me in their world. I was thrilled at first. Going to fancy-schmancy members' clubs, eating out at the best restaurants, drinking at secret bars or going to parties in million-pound penthouses. It sounds fabulous, right? And it was...for a minute. The thing about the filthy rich is that most of their conversations are fluff and fake. I appreciate these people for their nice clothes, their insane houses and their luxurious lifestyle. I had some fun moments, some good laughs. It was such a blissful momentary escape from my seemingly mundane life. My acting career had stalled and I just didn't want to think about it, so I thought hanging out with people who had money would help solve all my problems. It didn't, obviously.

What it did was make me realise this was not the life I wanted. I couldn't relate to any of these people and, to be honest, I didn't really want to. I didn't have anything in common with them. One night, we were all sitting at one of the best tables for the opening of a new restaurant in Mayfair. I was sitting amongst this loud group, all of them getting progressively drunker and louder, and I looked around and then looked at myself and didn't recognise the life I was living. It wasn't me. I was not a glitzy, glam, shallow girl, who enjoyed talking about money or parties without actually having to work or think about goals and dreams. I was a quiet, night in with a few friends, some wine and conversation kind of girl, someone who had big goals in life. How did I suddenly end up here, in an uncomfortable dress and killingly painful heels, watching people have way more fun than I was? To silence these thoughts, I decided to join in with the fun and stayed up drinking until 4 am. The next day was extremely painful.

I was insanely hungover and angry at myself. It was my fourth party of the week and not only was I feeling like hell, but it had finally occurred to me that I wasn't even sure I liked the people I was hanging out with at these parties. I barely knew them and the little I did know, I didn't like and couldn't relate to. How had this been going on for months without me realising I didn't enjoy it? I guess being caught up in the middle of the uber-rich, young heirs of South Kensington, going out to dinners, bars and clubs and not spending a cent will do that to someone. It does sound like a great life, doesn't it? Most people thrive in this world, so why was I feeling like crap? Didn't I want that life? Didn't I agree with these people's values and morals? Wasn't that glitzy life what everyone wants? What was up with me? And suddenly, this opened the gates to an overwhelming number of other questions.

I was lying on my bedroom floor, paracetamol in one hand, lemon water in the other, in the flat I had lived in for over six years, and my brain spiralled in a sea of questions. I questioned every single aspect of my life:

'Why am I dating this guy? Do I even want to date right now? Do I like sex? Do I want to fall in love? Do I want to be single? Why am I not progressing in my career? What is my purpose? What matters to me? What do I want? What makes me happy?'

And then it got weird. 'What's my favourite colour? Do I even have one? What clothes do I actually like wearing? What's my style? Do I like my job? Do I like living in London? Do I like this flat? Should I move to Australia and reinvent myself? Do I like my friends? What am I, outside of my job? What do I like? Do I like who I am? Who am I?'

It was endless. What a weird, intense day that was.

I mean, I wasn't buying a ridiculous car or destroying my soul with drugs, or whatever cliche looks like an identity freakout, but it was a crisis. It was a very stressful alarm bell with the main message being: WHO ARE YOU NOW? and WHY DON'T YOU KNOW?

I remember getting up, grabbing sheets of paper, sitting on the floor of my room and writing these questions down, questions I hadn't asked myself in years, some obvious and some not so obvious. Turns out my favourite colour had changed, but my dating habits hadn't. *This has been rectified since, thank you very much.* I wrote down what I thought were my qualities and faults, and not what I had heard other people say to me. I wanted to have a clearer vision of how I perceived myself and if it felt true at that moment. It took a minute to settle myself and answer these truthfully. I was mostly baffled that I had spent most of my twenties, going through life, not really thinking about these questions. But that moment was my brain's way of telling me, 'STOP. This is not the life you signed up for. This isn't you and this group of people is not good for you.'

What's important here is to realise that you have to make yourself a priority. For your own well-being and the people around you, you just have to. And if you end up being overwhelmed by millions of questions and identity freak-outs, don't panic. This is not a bad thing. This is just an opportunity to assess what's going on and if your choices are aligned with you. If the answer is no, then simply amend a few things. Check-in with yourself. Don't wait 28 years, like I did. It's not a nice feeling to be lost in your identity but I think it's a necessary one to give you a kick in the butt and get the ball rolling again. Press reset, start fresh, with a clearer idea of who you are and what you want out of this life.

This doesn't mean it won't happen again. Like I said, life moments can trigger identity questions. After a break-up, after a death, after a near-death experience, after an accident, after a fight, after having a baby, after watching a film, after listening to a song, after a trip. Anything, really. Try not to be too hard on yourself when it happens. It's OK to press pause on your life. Take a breather. Make yourself a priority and don't get too caught up in life, because life will catch up with you and it would be a shame to see that those choices were against who you were because you didn't stop to ask yourself if this was really you all along.

But here's the reassuring thing, and I really want you to hear me when I say this, *and please read it back whenever you feel like you are in a crisis*:

When you're in your twenties, *or at any point in life really*, there is this huge misconception that we are meant to know what the hell we're doing. This is WRONG. You are not meant to know everything all the time, ESPECIALLY in your twenties. My god. You do not have to have it all figured out by the time you're thirty. You do not have to be married, have kids and have a house by a certain age. That is bullshit. Some of the 59-year-olds I know don't have it figured out, so why the hell should your 29-year-old self have?? Makes zero sense. What you don't want to do is make choices out of what you think you're supposed to do because that just means you're creating a jail for yourself, and that's when crises occur; when you realise nothing aligned with what you wanted, or when some major event has shaken everything up and you realise you don't know who you are anymore.

When we talk about ourselves, it's sometimes really difficult to find perspective. That's why it can be a good idea to sit with yourself when you're feeling lost, confused or unsure about it all. *Don't feel the need to lie on the floor like I did, but I must say, there is something grounding about it.* We all feel it at some point. Writing down what is bothering you, and why, helps. We do have the answers, we just have to listen to what comes up. You're the only one who knows the answers about yourself, no one else. It might not always be pretty to come face to face with the shit you've been avoiding. But don't keep pushing it aside because you're only delaying the inevitable.

Regardless of the age, you might be at, if you don't really recognise yourself or you don't like the life you're living right now, then stop for a minute and ask yourself why, and what can be done about it. Because no matter what it is, there's a solution. You simply have to believe you deserve that solution and make it happen for yourself.

As a side note, I would also like to say: when things are going well, when you're feeling content, proud of where you're at, at ease, comfortable in yourself and your choices, happy with a decision that made you feel empowered, even though it was fucking hard, please take a moment and congratulate yourself, because that is bloody cool. Pat yourself on the back and treat yourself. What an accomplishment! Really feel that. Observe that journey, the growth. Those moments will make everything worth it, crises and all.

Just Be You: Flawed, Bold, Unique

"If it makes you happy, it doesn't have to make sense to others." – Anonymous

I had to remind myself of this quite a lot in my twenties. Everyone has a different idea of what happiness looks like and that's how it should be. Your life is not supposed to look or be like everyone else's. We make our own rules. However, there can be a time when you might be conflicted between being what the internet, society or your entourage say you should be, and simply being who you really want to be. It's a tough one. There's a lot of noise out there. A lot of potential comparisons to be made. Especially at a time when we get a glimpse into everyone's lives through social media.

What's damaging is that each person is fully in control of what they put out there, which means what we see online is, most of the time, the most amazing moments of our lives. The sunny holidays, the new babies, the weddings, the new jobs, the good angles, the filtered faces. It's relentless, unlimited information we can access at all times.

It is not *real*. It's very much fabricated. And yet, it creates this idea in our heads that our life should look like that. And if it doesn't, it can affect us on a daily basis. It's a reminder of what we don't have, even if we don't particularly want it. And that's dangerous because it can make you think you want something because social media is telling you it's good, as opposed to knowing what you *actually* want and what your true goals are in life. It's strange. It's all make-believe and yet we fully participate in it, every day, in a very addictive way.

I remember a few years ago, I had booked a great acting job and I was super happy. It wasn't a huge part, but it was a good part nonetheless. Well,

I went on social media and saw this girl, a stunning actress I used to do promo work with in London, post about the fact that she had just booked a lead role in a huge film and her boyfriend had proposed. Instantly, I felt like shit. I couldn't help it. That good feeling I had had a moment ago vanished because I felt like I would never be at her level, no matter how much I tried. It just reminded me that I was nowhere near that. It's awful because, had I not seen that post, I would've just been proud of myself and where I was at. But that one photo made me think that there are always going to be people ahead of the game, people who seem way happier than I am. It just sucks.

I had to take a break from it all. I had to remind myself of all the good things I had achieved every day and what I really wanted out of this life as opposed to what I was seeing online. Removing myself from social media did wonders to my mental health and overall mood. I wasn't looking into other people's lives, I wasn't missing out on anything, because I was way more present and supportive of myself without it. I went off social media for two months and came back to it with a new perspective.

The thing to remember about social media is that we post the best of our lives. I am guilty of it. I remember posting a smiley selfie I had taken on holiday after having been crying on the floor of my bedroom. No one would ever have had a clue. And you know what else? I bumped into this actress at an event, three months after that post, and it turned out her boyfriend had left her a month after that post and her lead role had been reduced to a smaller part. But she didn't post that, did she? Of course not. I couldn't believe that she was going through all of that and I had made up a whole other scenario in my head according to the five photos I had seen.

So please try to refrain yourself from comparing your life and where you're at to other people's lives. Every single person is on their own journey, walking their own path and heading towards their own destination. Focus on your own happiness, your own fulfilment, because it won't look like anyone else's. It shouldn't. Just keep walking in your own lane and do your own thing, at your own pace.

Being who you want to be is not always a walk in the park. Most of the time, we aim to please, right? We want people to like us. We want to leave a great impression. I'm guilty of that from time to time. And when the impression falls flat, it can feel devastating. There have certainly been times, especially in my early twenties, when I didn't feel that I was ever enough.

I have felt that regularly for years. I used to go to an acting class in London a few times a month. I loved it and hated it at the same time. I loved it because I got to act in a room full of talented actors. I hated it because I felt like I had something to prove as an actor and as a person every time I walked into that room. Not for myself, but for the other people watching. I wanted to leave an impression; I wanted to leave a mark. I wanted to nail it so people could be impressed. And I would usually go overboard. I would try and be a heightened version of myself instead of simply being me. My teacher finally called me out on it when I bumped into him at a cafe outside of class. He said to me, 'Ange, here we are, out of class and you're the funniest and most relaxed I've ever seen you. Where is that person in class? Why do I always sense you're putting on a character when you're in class?'

I told him that I felt like I had to be better than who I am. I was surrounded by such talent, I felt I really had to be 'ON' all the time in order to deliver in the room.

'Oh, that's bullshit,' he said. 'Next time I see you, I want you to let go of who you *think* you should be. Just be you, like you are now. Because that's where I see your unique charm come out.'

Funny enough, the next class is when I nailed the scene the most and made everyone finally laugh in a way I had wanted them to for months. A great impression had been made without me trying to be something I thought I was supposed to be.

So yeah, it's corny but here it is: being yourself is enough. Nothing less, nothing more. Just you. It will always be enough. There is no need to dim your light and there is no need to overdo it. Just be who you are, be happy with who this person is, and people will see that and respond to it positively. If you build up a facade or create another persona in a room, it won't be truthful and people won't engage with you as much because it won't feel honest.

My next point is: Be BOLD. This can be done in many different ways. But mostly, it's done by letting go of what people will think of you. I know, it's easier said than done. But really think about this. There is only one you. Only ONE. Isn't that a great feeling? How special is that? No one else can bring what you do to the table. But here's the thing, if you try to mould yourself to what everyone else considers normal, you're shaping yourself into something that isn't you. You're just trying to copy other people and that's no fun at all. That's no way to live. You're here to bring something unique to you and you should be proud of that. So be BOLD. And that goes in all areas of your life. Embrace your uniqueness, your quirkiness, your intelligence, your wit, and your sense of humour. You stand out by basically just being yourself, don't be afraid of it.

Do not worry what people think. If you are yourself and they don't like you, it's very much their loss. THEY miss out. You'll be ok because you're surrounded by people who get you, who like that person, the real you.

Personally, I am and have always been a little weird and I'm very aware that not everyone is going to like me. I'm loud, quite direct, brutally honest, stubborn, outspoken and a klutz. And that is ok. Not everyone HAS to like me. I'm loved by the best people, the people who understand me and who let me be that flawed person.

In high school, I used to wear these white go-go boots and neon green socks that were talked about by everyone in school. I loved dressing differently, I loved wearing flashy colours and fun clothes. And sure, it was a little extra, a little out there, *I have some killer group class photos to prove it,* but I also really didn't care what people thought. *The new teenager arriving from England in a French school, people were already talking.* However, it did give me a glimpse of how the world works and people's responses to it. It showed me who I was likely going to be friends with and who I was not going to engage with. Most girls didn't appreciate the attention I received and I had to learn that this might be the case as an adult as well. Some people don't respond well to boldness and creative unique choices. Especially when you come from a small town where everyone dresses the same. There can be a lot of jealousy, a lot of narrow-minded people or simply unhappy people who like to bully the happier ones. But here's the thing. Fuck 'em. I was entirely myself and happier than ever because I was just being me.

Don't worry, I'm not saying you have to dress in neon-green clothes, guys. But you can be bold in different ways, as long as it suits you. It doesn't mean you have to be outrageous. But come on, live a little! Take that trip you've been thinking about for ages, learn that instrument, ask that person out, wear bold lipstick, go back to school if you want a degree, dance it out in the supermarket aisle, take singing lessons... Do what makes you happy and confident, what suits you and only you. That's what people will remember you for. And if you fall flat on your face, *which I have physically and psychologically done multiple times*, you pick yourself up and try again. Make sure whatever you do is for YOU.

Which brings me to my final, most important, point.

Do not be afraid to fail. It is through failure that you find out who you are. This is one I had to learn the hard way. Nothing is ever pristine, easy or smooth-sailing. No matter how much you try. Sometimes, you have to go through the mud to figure out who you are. When you make mistakes, when you fail at something, when you take RISKS, you figure out how to pick yourself back up and that's when you see how you grow from that experience. It's what you do after the mistake that matters the most. That's when your true strength shines through. That's when life is really lived. Because without failures, you wouldn't recognise true success. Without feeling hurt or down, you wouldn't recognise happiness and fulfilment. It might shake you to your core, but it'll also make you realise you are stronger than you think. It'll push you to be a better person, a more fearless person. Trust me, one way or the other, you will benefit from those hurtful, painful moments in life.

Look at the people who have truly been successful in the world. They have achieved their success by being bold and brave. They took risks. They also fell down multiple times but they got back up and pushed through because they were themselves in a unique and inspiring way. It's worth it all.

And the thing is, not everyone is going to like you. Not everyone is meant to. It doesn't matter. YOU have to like you. And you won't be able to like yourself if you're putting on a character or if you're moulding yourself to fit into the crowd. So be who you want to be. Everybody else is taken, remember?

I may not have kept those white boots, *disgustingly over-worn,* but I will keep making those bold choices because boring is not the lifestyle I was ever meant to choose. *Just have a look at the Work chapter to see what I'm talking about.* And that's what suits me.

Please don't let anyone take that away from you. It is never worth it. Be bold, be brave enough to be yourself. Because that person is enough and will always be enough.

AUNTY ANGE TIPS

- Prioritise yourself. It is not selfish, it's vital.

- You don't want to just live, you want to thrive.

- Take a break from social media. Give it a week, a month, a few months. Everyone should do it to realise the answer is not online.

- Never put your happiness in someone else's pocket. Don't give anyone that power.

- Make decisions for your own happiness, not someone else's.

- Who you are is not a straight, simple road. It'll curve, hit dead ends, do a 360, have a few bumps and might even crash before starting up again. Just keep your hands on the steering wheel and you'll get there.

- Remove people who make you feel like you are not enough as you are. I mean it. Bye bye.

- Making lists of things you want and need, and questioning yourself, should never stop.

- No one else can tell you who you are, if they try to, tell them politely to Fuck off. *Politely.*

- If your identity crisis involves getting a tattoo, please try and think about the tattoo for a year, before engraving it on your skin. Just a thought.

- Don't be afraid to fail. It won't feel great for a minute but it's a right of passage and you will grow more from it. Promise.

Don't regret the different stages you've lived and gone through so far. Everything has led up to who you are now or will become.

III. LOVE

Welcome to the Love chapter. Boy, do you have a minute? I'm not really sure where to start with this one - it's *that* chaotic - but I'm going to try. First of all, I feel I should mention that during the course of writing my book, this particular chapter about my love life had to be revised a tremendous amount. I started writing it with a very cynical point of view about love, relationships and my experience of it all. It was full of terrible dates, awful sex, break-ups and images of dying alone with cats. *Uplifting stories, you know.*

However, in the course of writing the chapter, I..wait for it... fell in love. *Ew, I know.* Don't worry! I won't be going into a cheesy love fest. I'm just sayin', the uber cynical me has been softened a little. She's a little gentler and more open to the idea that not every guy on the planet is shit.

This does not mean that my love life didn't suck for most of my life, though. OK, that might be harsh, but it's not been great, folks. I take about 80 percent of the responsibility on this one. There have been several factors that contributed to the shambles that was my love life. Making excuses as to why it didn't work out with a guy is my forte. I'm an expert. I've pushed the right guys away and I've also trusted the wrong guys, shamelessly making excuses along the way. It's ok, I'm not judging myself, I'm just saying it as it is.

Everyone goes through life at their own pace, in their own time. When it comes to sex, love, settling down, breaking up, and finding love again, no story is the same. Which is why, as much as I can give advice here, everyone is going to feel differently when it comes to these topics – which actually goes for every chapter of this book.

What I can do is simply share how it all started and how it went down for me: my absolute worst dating stories in London, how to deal with sex, break-ups, commitment issues and upsetting disappointments. I also share some of the lessons learnt and suggest that maybe being open to finding real love is not impossible. We're going to get to the bottom of why my love life was the utter mess that it was – *enjoy* – and hopefully, you'll find some relatable moments, as well as some Ah ha! moments. Welcome to the madness. Enter at your own discretion.

At Your Own Pace

Let's get right into it.

If I tell you that my love life peaked in primary school and, for the next fifteen years, it went downhill from there, would you believe me? Just hear me out.

When I was eight years old, for Valentine's Day, a boy I really liked took me to the cinema and at the end of the film surprised me with a rose and a bracelet he had made out of string. He walked me home and kissed me on the cheek. When I moved away a few months later, he wrote me a letter that ended with: 'I will miss you, always.' I mean, come on! Does it get cuter than that? Granted, eight-year-old kids have it less messy than adults do, but still, that's as romantic as it gets, really. Compared to the rest of my love life in my twenties, that was pretty high up on the Sweet-Moments-With-The-Opposite-Sex list. I'm not saying there haven't been some romantic moments since then – it's not all been doom and gloom, thank goodness. But I do look back at my eight-year-old self and think 'Girl, you had no idea how precious, romantic and magical that was. It's about to get real messy.'

Let me walk you through it.

I started this book by saying that I've always been late to the party, literally and metaphorically. Aside from that beautiful, precious eight-year-old love story, I wasn't really in line with what everyone was focusing on as a teenager – meaning finding a person to kiss and fool around with.

Growing up, there is a tremendous amount of pressure to fit in and follow what everyone else is doing. Especially when it comes to dating and sex. I can only speak for myself, but I always felt like I was listening to everyone around me talk about something that I was just not interested in yet. I simply didn't get the appeal of being naked with a smelly, spotty high-schooler and telling all my friends about it. It was never really my aim to find a boyfriend at that time. I was focused on learning in school and having fun with my friends. And I did; I had a blast. But, you know, eventually, you see every other girl kissing guys and holding hands with someone, and it becomes the main topic of conversation; you think that's what you're meant to do. You're meant to follow this trend and show interest in guys – or girls.

So, at around 14 or 15 years old, I started dating. If I'm honest, I didn't care much about it and was nowhere near interested enough in sex to even remotely consider it, much to my mum's relief. Still, I was curious enough to play along and maybe *try* to like someone. *I know, that's not promising, is it?*

The first guy I started going out with was a year or so older than me and was really into this trendy dance called Tectonic, which blew up everywhere for a minute. *Google it, you won't regret it, it's utterly ridiculous.* For some unknown reason, I thought it was so cool to date someone a year older than me, who wore flashy-coloured clothes, *which I tragically matched with my own*, and who performed choreographed dance routines together, on our lunch breaks, in front of everyone in school. You should've seen us walk into school together, matching outfits and him always 'feeling the beat'. Horror. That should've been my first inkling that picking the right guy for me was just not going to be my strong suit in life. Looking back, I can't believe I even thought we were cool. *Come to think of it, I've decided I'm going to blame my friends for not stopping this flashy car crash immediately.*

Luckily, high-school choices don't follow you into adulthood unless of course you've fallen in love with your high-school sweetheart, married them and now have two beautiful kids together. *UGH, ew and congrats, I love that for you.* The Tectonic dude didn't last long and neither did the guy after that. When I think of high school, I mostly think of all the parties and fun nights out with my friends. Occasionally kissing boys in clubs or drunkenly spinning that bottle at house parties and moving on. I kept it light and fun. Maybe deep down, I was a bit scared of it becoming anything serious. I certainly didn't feel ready to have sex yet. High school ended and I gladly only have amazing memories of being young, free and surrounded by friends. I guess I also remained fairly innocent of what was to come when relationships actually got serious. So, I left school unscathed, scarred only by the stress of exams and the many drunken tumbles I endured during my nights out.

It's not like there weren't opportunities to have sex. There were many opportunities where I could've slept with someone. It just never felt like the right time or person. During the summer, I used to make crepes in this little stand on the beach. *I know, I could not be more French.* The lifeguards were right opposite me and obviously, I ended up dating one of them. *Oh don't give me that look, you would've too. I kind of wish I had slept with the Baywatch guy, mostly because that would've been such a good story to tell.*

We went out a few times but it didn't lead anywhere. Sex was yet to be had for this 17-year-old chick.

At university, everything was still very much vanilla for me. I partied a lot, kissed many frogs, drank crappy, cheap wine, and studied occasionally. I definitely could have slept with someone back then, but again, I didn't find the guy I was ready to do it with. I was getting progressively pickier. Didn't mean I didn't want to have sex, though. Don't get me wrong, this gal was 19 years old and ready to do the deed. I guess I just had this ideal image in mind. And let me tell you, it ended up being anything but ideal.

I moved to London when I was 19 and I definitely felt, by that point, that after two years at university and dating guys, I just needed to get it over with. Everyone around me seemed to have had sex and whether I admitted it to myself or not, that bothered me. So what did I do? I slept with the completely wrong dude – the first one I dated in London. He was 10 years older than me and owned this swanky flat in Kensington. We had known each other for about two weeks and on our third date, he took me to his place. I don't remember much of that evening. I think it might be that selective memory we sometimes hear about. I remember us randomly watching Ocean's 11. I remember me eating most of the popcorn and as I was going in for more, suddenly he was kissing me and it went from there. The guy had NO idea what he was doing. It was tragic. It lasted about five minutes and it was so underwhelming that I remember sitting on the toilet thinking, 'What the fuck was that? I waited 19 years for this?'

I don't have many regrets in life, but I do wish I had waited a bit longer, waited for someone who knew me longer than those two bloody weeks, someone who could've made me feel the way a girl is supposed to feel during sex. I had waited for 19 years and somehow felt like I had had to get it done with the first dude I dated in London. It's a common thing, I hear. *He did ruin Ocean's 11 for me though. And seeing how hot Brad Pitt is in that film, it's a real shame...Moving on.*

Many years later, while talking about our first times with my girlfriends, I found out that I wasn't the only one to have this kind of experience. Not even close. Most of our first times are crap. It's not pleasant. Even when it's with someone right! So do not judge yourself for how it went, who with, or at what age. I thought I was being smart, waiting to be ready, and look what happened. Just because I put pressure on myself, I slept with a dude I never even saw again.

So, if any of you gals out there are feeling that pressure to have sex or if someone is pressuring you before you feel ready, remind yourself that every single person is different and if you're not ready, then you're not ready. The right person will come along. Be patient, be smart and respect yourself enough to wait for the right moment.

I let myself be so focused and consumed by the idea of having sex that I didn't really think of the aftermath and what it would mean afterwards. I wish I could've told my younger self that there was no shame in waiting.

Because there isn't. Also, if you happen to have had an awful, premature, awkward, shitty first time, then welcome the club! There are thousands of us. You live and learn and pass wisdom, am I right?

Once the Losing Your Virginity is out of the way, this doesn't mean that sex is suddenly an easy, smooth sailing experience with everyone you date. No, no. There's a period of figuring out where you stand with having sex in general. Like I said, you make up your own rules, in your own time.

When I was in my early twenties, I always felt like we had to rush to the sex part of the relationship quite quickly. A friend of mine told me one day that she had been dating this amazing guy for about a month and it was going really well. I asked her how the sex was and she said she hadn't slept with him yet. I was shocked. Clearly, I had lived in London too long where everything moves at such a rapid pace. I couldn't understand at first why, if she liked the guy, she hadn't slept with him yet and also, how was he still AROUND. Isn't the guy going to lose interest? Aren't people meant to have sex in the first few weeks of dating? She explained that it was something she was trying. She wanted to build intimacy elsewhere first because she liked him and didn't want to rush into quite an important step. 'Not everything is about sex', she told me. And that was a real eye-opener. You can have sex when you decide and when you feel it's right.

This also means that you can have sex on a first date if you feel like it. A friend of mine is terrified of the penis size issue. Having dealt with an alarming amount of micro-penises in her life so far, waiting a month to see the guy's penis isn't something she'd agree to. Each to their own, people! No rules, no judgement, just feeling what's right for you.

As I continue on the subject of 'rushing into things.' I would say the same thing applies when it comes to entering the Serious Relationship zone. There is no need to move at warp speed when it comes to committing to someone or settling down. And yes, this may be coming from someone who is quite a commitment freak, I'm not denying that, but I have learned that it's OK to make up your own rules as you go. It's really important to not abide by everyone else's choices. There are fewer and fewer rules when it comes to living together, being engaged for longer, and having kids without being married. It's a different time from when our parents were ticking all those boxes before turning 25. Going at your own speed also means that if you think things are going too fast in your relationship, you are entitled to slow it down and take baby steps. If you are with the right person, there won't be any need to speed through those steps, if you're planning to stay the rest of your lives together that is. And if you are with the right person, I have found that those steps become less scary, especially if you're with someone that respects your boundaries and considers your needs.

I'm not saying some steps won't be scary, though! The I love yous, the moving-in chats, meeting the family, marriage plans – it can all be absolutely terrifying. And when it comes to relationships, I find EVERYTHING terrifying. There is so much to learn in that fear. Being in a relationship has taught me more than I ever thought it would. The sweetness, the disappointments, the messiness, the insecurities, the good, the bad, the falling in love, and the facing the fear of climbing over that big wall I had built around myself. It's a lot, for anyone. You simply have to be open and ready for it. In one's own time.

Relationships: Learning From Them, Being Open to Love

So, 20-year-old me had popped her cherry. And it was not as glorious as she hoped. The irony is, I found a wonderful guy a few months later, which goes to show that patience really could've come in handy when I was obsessing about getting it over with, with Mayfair Dude.

Indeed, four months after the Ocean's 11 five-minute sex fiasco, I went back to France to spend some time at home, recovering from the brutal experience of being new in London, with no money and no clue about anything in life. I wasn't planning on meeting anyone, quite the opposite. My idea of sex had been quashed and I was just looking to forget the whole experience. However, as the hypochondriac that I am, I thought I might have to go on the pill, in the eventuality that I might have – hopefully, better – sex again. *I am getting somewhere with this story, don't you worry.* So, one morning, I went to the pharmacy to get this prescription and there was a new pharmacist there. Very handsome man. I was completely taken aback. It's a small town and I thought I had met everyone worth meeting at that point. This guy was new and that was exciting. As I was speaking to him, rambling on and attempting to seem normal, I managed to glance at his name tag and mentally made a note of his name, Pierre.

That evening, I was explaining the story to my best mates and we drunkenly ended up finding him on Facebook. We decided, *ok ok, I decided*, three glasses of wine in, that it would be a brilliant idea to message him. Much to my surprise, he messaged back and asked me out. And that was the beginning of our relationship. It would've been quite easy to tell you that that was the end of the story, we lived happily ever after. But no. I was not going to make my life that predictable.

Nope, basically, I decided that this perfect guy I was dating was not going to make the cut, because why make life so easy, right? In all fairness, it didn't work out for many valid reasons, one of which was that I went back to London for work and the long-distance relationship thing involved a ton of effort. Efforts I was not willing to prioritise over my new career. I simply couldn't invest as much time in the relationship as he wanted me to. That's the reason I gave, anyway. I now know, deep down, as much of a saint as he was, I just wasn't in love and was, in fact, terrified of the idea. So, what do you do when you're scared? You find ways to push that person away. The defence mechanism, I have since mastered over the years, really started growing legs with him, the lovely French doctor man. *It's not a particularly nice technique and one I wouldn't promote, by the way.*

I remember one night we were walking home after a perfectly lovely evening that I somehow managed to be unappreciative of. It started pouring rain and I was pissed off about something. *I can guarantee you it was probably about something uber nice he had said or done...ISSUES, GUYS, I had issues.* He stopped in the middle of the road and told me he loved me. I really couldn't believe him. I couldn't understand how a person could love me when all I had done was try to push them away. And what did I do then? I got angry. I got so frustrated with him. I wasn't ready for someone to love me. I wasn't ready to let someone in. But no one teaches you that stuff. I had no idea why I wasn't jumping up and down at the sight of a lovely, available man saying he loved me. I've seen all the movies; I thought I could do it. Turns out, looking back, I didn't love myself enough back then to let someone else love me. I had my own shit to deal with first. I had so much growing up to do and the fact that a guy saying 'I love you' made me want to throw up was definitely a sign I couldn't be in a relationship then. I'd like to say my commitment issues have evaporated since but keep reading. I think you'll find that commitment is still quite a triggering concept for me, even years later. *Maybe for you too? No? You got everything sorted? Fuck...*

I owe the Doc a lot, though. First of all, that one year together redeemed any bad experience I had had before. I learned a lot about having to care and think about someone else's feelings above my own, which is something you can only really figure out when you're with someone. No one can teach you that part. I learned that caring about someone and being in love with them are two different things. I learned that pushing people away is an act of fear – the fear of catching feelings and being hurt. And it's only when you look back on those kinds of experiences years later that you realise it was never meant to be. It was meant to be a great story at that moment and stay there in the past.

I have nothing bad or unpleasant to say about that year. He was wonderful and frankly, if I had known about all the other loser guys I was going to encounter after him, I may have given the relationship a longer shot. *Although, it would've made this chapter of the story far less exciting and hilarious for you guys.* Truth is, you can't force a relationship if you are not ready for it. No matter how great the other person is, working on yourself matters and I knew, at that time, that working on my issues was the priority over having a serious boyfriend. That relationship also showed me the *amount* of work I had to do on myself before even considering being in a serious, committed relationship again. It wasn't a soul-destroying break-up, but it was an eye-opener for me.

The unpleasantness came in my second relationship.

Unpleasant but, man, was there Growth there. This is definitely where I learned the most, about myself, about what I wanted out of a partner but also how the other person's maturity and honesty, really matter to make it work and align with your wants.

When I was around 26 or 27, I felt I was ready to maybe try the relationship thing again. Dating can be tedious – *get ready for those stories below* – and I knew stability would be welcome at that time in my life. I wasn't really looking for it, but a nice guy came my way and successfully wooed me. For months, we were having a great time. We seemed to want the same things, and we saw each other regularly but also had our own lives. I introduced him to my mother and he even managed to fool her. Everything was just smooth sailing. Until it wasn't. Out of the blue, he said he couldn't do it anymore – in a text, might I add – and disappeared. He didn't reply to my messages and unfollowed me on everything. I was very shocked and, as much as I hate to say it, very hurt. The one feeling I had tried to avoid for so long hit me in the face with no warning or explanation. It just sat there, in my body, for a while. Those 'Break-Up playlists' on Spotify really were the bane of my existence for a minute there. What is tricky with situations like these is that there was no closure. He didn't explain, he didn't even say it face to face. He sent a text and vanished. Nowadays, you would call this term 'ghosting'. Although, as I understand it, ghosting doesn't even involve a text. They become a GHOST. Which did feel quite similar.

I felt stupid, I'm not going to lie. I felt that the whole relationship had been a complete waste of time and, for someone who says they can read people well, I had been completely misled and tricked. I wish I could say it ended there. But this is where I learnt my true lesson: Ghoster Boy came back. Crawling. He called me a couple of months after disappearing, saying he wanted to talk face-to-face and explain himself. Now, I pride myself on being a very stubborn, independent, 'if you hurt me, you're dead to me' kind of gal, but because I am also someone who needs an explanation – or at least closure – I agreed to hear him out.

He explained that he got really scared of his feelings for me and was overwhelmed by us being serious. Now, I know exactly how this sounds. I'm the first one to say it when I see it with other people. Cowards aren't usually welcome in my world. I like someone who can be honest about their feelings and tell me straight up what's going on. But I also completely knew what he meant when he said he was scared of his feelings. I had been there. So, I surprised myself. I decided to give him the benefit of the doubt and try again.

But it turns out, once you hurt me, I can't go back and forget. Something had been broken, and as much as I wanted to be the bigger person and forgive, I didn't feel good about doing it. I didn't feel like he deserved me anymore. And so, much to my surprise again, I chose to honour myself. I chose to end it. On my terms.

Not only had I discovered that I had firm boundaries, but I knew that they had been overstepped.

Boundaries. It's important to have them, it's important to be aware of what yours are. Something in me clicked then and I knew that I had to draw a line in the sand. Guys, and girls, will test boundaries. It's all part of the game, it's part of discovering each other. Sometimes, boundaries will be overlooked or trampled on. It's your job to show up for yourself, know your limits and put your foot down when they are not being respected or when you feel you're being pushed over what you wanted. In this case, I decided to prioritise myself and my happiness. I knew that I couldn't move past that disrespectful ghosting situation and the trust that had been broken.

It is important to know what is best for you. Even when you care dearly about the person. There's that beautiful quote by Tara Westover: 'You can love them and still choose to say goodbye. You can miss them every day and still be glad they are no longer in your life.'

It's gutting but some choices have to be made for your own well-being, above everyone else's. If you manage to do that for yourself, that's the kind of strength some people only dream of having. Pat yourself on the back.

However, there is a point to be made about forgiving someone who has hurt you and maybe giving them a second chance. Every situation and every person is different. My experience is one of many different stories. A big lesson for me here was to not judge when someone takes their partner back after a bad experience. I used to really struggle with the idea of a girl taking a cheating guy back. Forgiveness is a really powerful thing and sometimes it can work for you. Other times, too much has been broken. But you and only you will know if you can overcome that challenge. Going through that, and taking him back after being hurt, is something I never thought I'd do. I didn't even think I'd consider it and yet, I did. For a brief time. So, never judge a woman, or a man, for making a decision you might not have made. Everyone is entitled to their own choice. It wasn't easy but I knew that I had to walk away. Making that decision, as tough as it was, was truly empowering. I truly think I came into my own. I was putting myself first and I was very proud of that.

It was only after that relationship ended that I realised I had just gone through the one thing I had been terrified of since I was 20. I had been hurt by someone else. I had finally let someone in and they had disappointed me.

But guess what? I survived. I came out the other side with some experience, wisdom and more clarity on what I will and won't tolerate. I became more aware of what I deserve and decided to not settle for less. Turns out, being hurt was pretty much the best thing that could've come my way at that time. It made me understand that I could survive it and that I could appreciate that relationship for the lesson it was. Trust the process and learn from your past relationships. They give us tools to be better and want better things for us in the future.

I try not to be resentful of my past relationships. After all, I chose to be with those people and they've all helped me become the person I am today. That's the mature way of putting it. Of course, I've had moments of 'Gosh remember that time I dated that loser, WTF was that about?' Some guys aren't going to serve any purpose at all, apart from just being a weird blip in your story. Nothing wrong there. Let's just focus on the good stuff here, OK?

My biggest fear was and has always been: once you're hurt, assuming you get hurt, or disappointed, how can you trust people again? How can you let someone in again? Well, I don't have a clear answer. I was and still am quite a guarded person, although I have definitely worked on that over the years. When you are so used to building a wall, creating a hard shell and blocking love from coming your way, it is very difficult to break those habits. Letting myself be completely open to love, being loved and trusting that process with someone took a long time.

Being open to love is accepting to be vulnerable with someone and that takes guts – I wasn't ready for it until the year I turned 30. That's right, during the course of writing this book, I fell in love. Hard. That big love you see in movies. I realised it was something I hadn't let myself do until now. It wasn't something I had been close to finding. I hadn't been ready. A reminder that TIMING is everything. It is key. Funny enough, I had met this gorgeous, kind man when I was 25 and we had even gone on a couple of dates. *He says it was three dates and we will never agree on this. Let's move on. Love you baby.* We definitely liked each other back then but the timing wasn't right. It simply wasn't our time. But somehow, during the year I turned 30, the year I had said out loud that I was ready for something real, five years after we met, he popped back into my life and we were both ready for our story. *Is this making you look into your dating history, checking if you missed anyone? Ha, my plan is working.*

Things usually happen when they are meant to happen when the person is ready for it. It's about trusting that everything happens at the right time for everyone. I was ready but scared. Even when this man came along, it took a minute for me to open up. It took patience from him and taking myself out of my comfort zone in order to get there.

Breaking those walls is truly wonderful. I've never experienced anything like it. It feels magical. But it's SCARY. No one really tells you or can prepare you for that. It won't ever stop being scary. You're opening yourself up to many amazing feelings but that vulnerability means you're opening yourself up to potentially being hurt. We do this ON PURPOSE, guys. We know it could come. At any point. And yet, it's LOVE, so how can you not? You can't put a price on that. It's probably going to be worth the risk. Facing your fears will only lead you to better things. Some moments and feelings are irreplaceable. On the other side of the wall I had built over many years, there was a whole world of feelings and wonder. It bears saying though that, as a former cynical dating frenzy chick, saying these things would've sounded very unnatural even a year ago. *When you read about the absolute shitshow of dates I have been on, the idea of love and lifelong happiness with someone would've made me gag a little.*

I am very grateful I managed to get there because it really is what everyone says. *I also think my grandmother is extremely relieved I won't die alone with cats. I think the whole family is, actually.*

I'm not saying opening yourself up to love is an easy task. Especially when you've been hurt before. It's a tough one. But I'm going to say the cheesy thing here: time heals most things. Time will help most wounds and you will come out stronger on the other side. Being hurt does not mean you should give up on finding love. I used to think that. I used to think that I would never let myself go through that disappointment again and if that had to mean, building walls and closing my heart, so be it. Here's the thing, that's not a way to live. You certainly don't need a man or a woman to complete you. Many women and men I know have amazing lives that are not defined by a partner. And that is their choice. But *deliberately* shutting yourself out of feeling love because you're scared of a negative outcome isn't a happy choice. It's a choice made out of fear of the future, and that is never going to lead to anywhere fulfilling. Enjoy the ride you're on, enjoy the process – in the *present* moment.

My approach to dating and love was not really the healthiest in my twenties. I equated feeling for someone to some sort of danger in my head. *That and simply not being ready for love or being in a committed relationship.* One thing I will say is: thinking that if you don't catch feelings you don't get hurt, leads to literally nowhere. You miss out on the good stuff by doing that and you only end up hurting yourself. You are certainly allowed to be your own shield and look out for yourself, but you gotta let through the people that matter, the people who show you they care, the people who love you. It feels so good when you allow yourself to feel that love coming at you. You just have to let it in for the right person. And the right person will come along when you're ready to let that guard down and feel it all.

OK! Let's cool it on the relationship talk. Frankly, I don't know enough about the subject to keep going on for this long. *Imposter syndrome is kicking in.*

Let's talk about DATING. This is where I shine. *Shine in absurdity.* More precisely, where my dating history sparkles. *Sparkles with wacky, ridiculous stories.*

Being Single: A Glimpse Into the Dating World

If you do the 'dating thing' right, it can be fun, freeing, and experimental. Dare I say, if you're feeling a little bit in a rut, it can spruce your life right back up... OR if that fails, you can pretty much guarantee that it'll attract messy, absurd and hilarious stories, just like the ones I'm about to share with you. *You're welcome.*

Between the relationships, I had seven *glorious* years of dating, on and off. Dating is very much part of the London culture and was certainly a big part of my life in the city. Coming from a small town in France, I never thought I'd enjoy the dating scene. Turns out, I learned how to have fun, and be free – and I've collected a few tragic and weird dating stories along the way.

Dating apps have helped diversify the dating scene. I fought against them for so long, wanting the organic, natural meeting you see in movies, but eventually, I caved. It turns out that there is nothing wrong with online dating. You get to meet people in different fields, different areas, people you'd never cross paths with in normal ways. It also means you're going to encounter a wider range of men/women, some for you, some not quite up your alley. And damn, have I met some weirdos. Enough to make me want to give up on men altogether at one point. I'm glad I didn't... *I guess I'm a more hopeful person than I thought.*

Allow me to tell a few of my best stories. I like to think that wherever you might be in this department, this WILL make you feel better about your dating lives. Here we go:

In first place, we have: Fleeing Man. This was a casual first date. He seemed fairly normal in his texts. *I'm now fully aware that that means Jack shit.* It was summer, and I chose a pub with a lovely outdoor terrace, so we could sit in the sun. Cute, right? I arrived at the pub and the guy is sitting in the darkest, coldest corner of the terrace in the shade, beer already in hand. Major red flag already, but this was still in the early days of my dating app scene, so I didn't think much of it. I approached him and said, 'Oh could we maybe sit in the sunshine since it's a lovely evening?' He mumbled something, got up and chose a different table in the sun without saying anything. We sat down and didn't talk for about 30 seconds. *Which is a fucking long time especially when I'm dead sober, with no drink in hand.* I knew I had to start a conversation. And here's something you might need to know about me: when I see someone nervous, I try to make them feel more comfortable by rambling on FOREVER. Non-stop. Which is what I did...for 25 minutes. He didn't order me a drink or even offer to. But what I did notice was the entire label of his beer being nervously peeled off, shredded into tiny pieces, scattered all over the table. After 25 minutes, I gave up trying and said 'Listen, should we maybe just go?' He said OK, got up and started walking out of the pub quite quickly, at an alarmingly rapid pace. I did my best to keep up with him. I asked if he was OK and he said, 'Well it's just... you're quite intimidating.' Which made me stop in my tracks, *quite out of breath trying to keep up with him.* I was baffled. I had spent the past half an hour trying to make this guy comfortable with my shitty jokes and life stories. I was kind of offended and annoyed. So, I joked: 'OK, fine, go then, run, run away!' The guy took this opportunity to... wait for it... SPRINT OFF. Like... PHYSICALLY run away from me. I turned around thinking that maybe someone was pranking me, but no. Dead serious. I just stopped, watching this guy sprint away into the sunset, like his life depended on it. I burst out laughing and walked home thinking that was the most wasted 30 minutes of my life. *I do wonder what happened to him sometimes. Maybe he's still running.*

Sit tight, I've got a whole bunch of these. We have the guy who spoke in a high-pitched monotone voice, was vegan and told me I was a murderer if I ate meat.

One guy thought that the idea of a perfect spot to try to kiss me was next to the pile of stinky bins in Soho Square. He kissed me with zero warning while I was mid-conversation and I was so surprised that I pushed him away and... well, you guessed it, he fell into the pile of bins.

We have Claude-Paul who took me to a Michelin-starred restaurant because he wanted to tick off all the four Michelin-starred restaurants in London before he turned 35. He spent £300 on the meal but didn't want to take the Underground home because he had never used it... Ugh, the rich can be gross sometimes. *But also, you name your kid Claude-Paul, you're asking for it.*

Of course, I had a guy who lied about his height, and clearly had some sort of unfinished business with his brother – who apparently ruined his childhood by calling him fat and ugly – since he felt compelled to tell me why he was no longer fat in the first 30 minutes of our date.

Shall I keep going?

One fella looked 20 years older than his photos, had lost most of his hair and was clearly going through some sort of mental breakdown. He spent the first hour talking about how the whole year had been super tough on him – his two dogs had just died as well as his dad. *The dead dogs were mentioned before the dead dad, might I add.* On top of that, his favourite food was tuna pasta. *What?* He also thought my accent was 'a bit Irish'. When I told him I was English and French, he said 'Ah yeah that makes sense, my hearing is really bad.'

Finally, we have a real special dude, a gem of the dating scene. Get ready. This guy seemed actually OK. He looked like his photo, was cute, could hold a conversation and had a job. *Fucking hip-hip hurray, right?* He had picked a nice place, the date was going swimmingly but towards the end of the meal, when it was about 9:30 p.m., he kept looking at his watch and seemed kind of in a rush to get home. I could not figure out why. We didn't have spicy or unusual food, so that was food poisoning out of the question. He kept looking at his phone and my thought immediately went to 'Oh here we go, he's got a girlfriend waiting at home or a wife and kids.' When we got to the tube station, I asked him why he was in such a hurry to leave, when we seemed to be having a good time. He got quite serious and nervous all of a sudden. I was prepared for anything. After eight years in London, very little fazes me anymore. The guy was probably going home to a pregnant woman or lived in his mum's basement.

Anyway, after about a minute of wondering if he should tell me, he decided to come clean. He lifted his left trouser up to show me his ankle. I was very confused at first and then, that's where I saw...drum roll please... an ANKLE MONITOR. Turns out, the guy was on probation and had a curfew. He had to get home before 10:30 pm for the next eight months. No joke. I speechlessly walked away and didn't speak to him again. My only regret is not asking him what he had done. I guess I didn't have it in me and funny enough, I didn't really feel like dating a criminal. Call me vanilla, that's where I draw my line.

And that's it on FIRST dates. *Yeah, we haven't even got to the second or multiple dates part of it yet.* Welcome to living in the big city. You simply multiply the loonies and somehow become more immune to anything weird. It's my superpower. Unflinched by nut-jobs. *Should I add that to my resume?*

I'm going to get to the nicer parts of dating in a second but I feel I just need to exorcise the gloomy stuff first. *Get it off my chest, you know.* So if by some miracle, you find yourself having a successful first date, congratulations.

Welcome to Level 2 of Dating Jumanji. You are now in a promising phase. There is hope. The guy seems fairly normal, there's conversation there. We can work with this.

Well, don't speak too soon. I've got another good one for you. I once met this perfectly normal guy and the first date had gone well. Jokes were flying, there seemed to be chemistry. A second date was planned quite quickly at a lovely Greek restaurant. No red flags yet. The date went smoothly and I was starting to think there could be potential there. We finished our meal. I went to the toilet before leaving, came back and he said we were good to go, all sorted. I waved at the hard-working staff. *Always be nice to your waiters, folks, that job is HARD.* We arrived in front of the station in Leicester Square. I proceeded to thank him for a wonderful dinner and this is where he, very proudly, tells me he didn't pay. I thought he was joking, so I laughed. An awkward few seconds passed and I said: 'WHAT?' He continued, 'Yeah they were taking ages and they didn't notice, so I thought it was funny to just leave.'

Now, having been a waitress myself, I know that if your table does a runner, you will get in trouble. No doubt about it. I was fuming. I can still picture the smug look this idiot had on his face. Unsurprisingly, with my track record, in the middle of that awkwardness, he thought it would be acceptable to try and kiss me. I pushed him away and left, blocking him from my contacts and brain. For two days, I couldn't sleep knowing that a waiter would have paid for that idiot's action. So, I dragged myself back to the restaurant and explained the situation to the judgy-looking manager, who recognised me instantly. She told me it actually was the waiter's first shift there and he had had to give his tips that night. *Dig me a deeper hole.* I paid for the tips, and as I left, she told me 'Make sure you bring a decent man next time.' I didn't date for a while after that one, which, in all honesty, was necessary.

The sign of all signs that I was starting to date a little too much was the day I was working at the door of an event and a guy I had been on a few dates with, six months prior, turned up with his girlfriend. He said hello to me. I looked at him blankly for a solid 10 seconds, not having a CLUE who he was.

Instead of pretending he got it wrong and that we didn't know each other, he insisted that we rehash details of our dates and even asked me if I remembered his name...in front of everyone, including his uncomfortable girlfriend.

I told him I didn't remember. He replied: 'It's Mark.' I replied, 'Oh yes, that's right, of course, Mark!' He then finished with, 'It's George actually. Have a good night.'

Safe to say, the universe gave me a clear sign that I needed to cool it on the serial dating frenzy that had become my life.

So, yes, dating in London has been both entertaining and complete chaos. There's no other way to describe it. I've kissed a lot of frogs. Not to say that I haven't dated wonderful guys, I definitely have. *Hi guys!* It's just more fun to talk about the worst dates rather than the ones that actually go smoothly, don't you think?

I like to think I have lived my twenties just as I thought I would. I don't think I was ever meant to settle down in my twenties. I wasn't built that way. I think I just knew that it wasn't my priority to find the man I was going to spend the rest of my life with. I was going to work on myself first. Be a whole person first. Be complete on my own, and that took working on myself and getting to know myself on my own.

Someone once told me, when I was in my early twenties, not to be in a relationship with anyone I wouldn't marry. That stuck with me. I mean, not to sugar-coat it, but... it's kind of a waste of time and it takes you off the market! I was focused on building friendships. I knew I shouldn't worry too much about relationships at that time of my life. My twenties weren't spent trying to fall in love or worrying about having a partner. They were spent on me, on finding myself. And so that's what I let happen. Most of my dating experiences have involved being with a guy for a few months, having a good time and then coming to some sort of understanding that it wasn't not going to work out. For various reasons: I didn't want it to get too serious, there wasn't any spark, I got bored, I was travelling too much to make it work, I wasn't ready, bad timing, they turned out to be nut cases or I simply didn't have or want to give it the time it needed. It's important not to be too hard on yourself in those moments. Things sometimes just don't work out. And why force something that isn't really there?

In our twenties, it can feel like there's quite a lot of pressure to get things right, to know what we want and that is that. I don't believe that's true. It's important to ask yourself what you want but you don't have to KNOW for sure. And maybe you find out that what you thought you wanted isn't the right thing for you. No big deal. You're meant to explore in your twenties. You are allowed to change, it's part of the process. We evolve. See what sticks and what doesn't. That's what dating gave me. It was a massive eye-opener. I know that, at times, I had no clue what I was looking for. There was a lot of back and forth in my brain sounding a lot like this: 'Don't settle down, your twenties are there to have fun and make the most of it... but don't you want to come home to something stable and comforting?' Then back to 'But I don't want to be hurt, I like having my freedom, I like being single too...but I want to fall in love.' – and so on. It's just a mess. It's been chaotic in my brain, no doubt about it. But how can it not be? We change so much from when we are 20 to when we are 29, sometimes it's just hard to keep track of ourselves *all* the time!

Ultimately, I've always pictured my twenties as a decade where I was going to have fun, experiment, be free and experience as much as I could. That's how I envisioned it, and I like to think I succeeded in that respect. I learned so much about myself in the many terrible, ridiculous dates I've been on, standing my ground and growing my standards.

This also brings me to this very important point: I think being single at certain periods in your life is the best thing you can do for yourself and your growth. I'm not saying dump whoever you are with now, but being single should be part of the journey of self-discovery. Because at the end of the day, you need to figure out how to be whole on your own before letting someone into your life. It's important to be comfortable on your own. Embrace it fully. If you are looking for someone to complete you, you are on the wrong track. YOU complete you. I wish this was taught to young girls early on. You do not need a man to fulfil you. Being with someone is a lovely, magical bonus because loving someone is pretty great, but you can shine just as bright on your own. And allowing yourself to be single, and seeing what you find out about yourself, will only make your future relationships better because you will have a better understanding of who you are outside of a relationship.

Being single doesn't mean you have to be *completely* on your own. Go on dates! Figure out what you like and don't like. Find out what your standards are and do that by listening to YOU. I know it can be noisy out there. People's life choices can affect our own path...if we let them.

People are always going to have opinions about your life, but you should never let them guide your decisions. There's always going to be that aunt who tells you that you might be too picky, or a grandma who keeps saying she wants to live to be a great-grandma... *I know Mamie, I know!*

Some people are made to be in relationships and thrive that way. My high-school best friend met her guy at 21 and she's now 30, living with him in a house they built, with a beautiful baby girl. And that works for her. For them. It wasn't for me; it was never going to be me. It wasn't what I wanted out of my twenties. Which is why most of my twenties were full of short-lived relationships. I learned more about myself that way. And had a hell of a lot of fun along the way. *Criminal guy aside, of course.*

Some people would look at my dating history and say I've dated casually to keep people at arm's length and maybe that's true. Dating is super fun and very freeing. It can become a bit of an endless game, though. You get to meet lots of different people, go to plenty of cool places and have a good time. It's light and most of the time, painless. However, sometimes you lose track of what it is you're actually looking for. That mindset does make you forget sometimes, or at least it did for me – that maybe having something stable is an option. Maybe it would be nice to be steady with one person. Why not? Again, you're allowed to change your mind, to evolve, to mature. Nothing is set in stone.

There certainly came a point for me where casual dating wasn't doing as much for me anymore. When the idea of being a bit more serious with someone became more appealing, and that's when I knew I was ready for it. I just had to pay attention to that feeling. BUT let's face it. Dating ain't no picnic. You have to be patient with it, with yourself and with finding the right person at the *right* time. That's a process too.

If you're single in a big city, trying to have a thriving career, juggling a social life and trying to find love, it's not an easy one to navigate. TIMING. Everyone has various priorities at any given time. You need to know what you want and then find a person who wants those similar things at the same time. TIMING is key here. I've met some really awesome guys who were very much ready to settle down when I was not even remotely there yet. And sometimes, it was the opposite. It just means you're not in the same place mentally. TIMING. It's everything. It also means you can meet the right person at the wrong time. I think we all know that from looking at Jennifer Aniston and David Schwimmer, no? *DAMN IT, you guys!*

Just don't be too hard on yourself. If it is meant to happen, it will happen. If you want to stay single, do it. If you want to casually date, be my guest. Don't settle for anything less than what works for you. Why would you? This is your life. And we all have busy lives! We need to make sure all the components contribute positively to our lives and not the opposite. If you're going to allow someone in, make damn sure they are a bonus, that they aren't a heavy weight around your neck.

In the meantime, I hope I haven't scared you on the subject of Dating. It was a little glimpse into the wonders of it. Granted, my journey has been very eclectic but I wouldn't trade it.

And that's just the dating part. You can have great dates, ones that give you hope... Wait 'til we get to the sex part. The terrible, forgettable sexual experiences we have all encountered as young adults. The sleeping with someone and wondering if you'll ever have mind-blowing sex, more than every five years?

Brace yourselves, we are now entering a non-PG 13 segment I like to call:

Sex: The Good, the Great, the WTF

Sex is a very interesting beast to discover in your twenties. I don't think it is really ever 100 percent figured out. What I do know is that the many years of casual dating in London and growing into my own person definitely helped evolve the relationship I had with sex and the way I feel about it now. In ways I didn't really expect.

So, this might not be that uncommon but I'm saying it anyway: I personally didn't really enjoy sex for the first few years of having it. I just didn't get it. Not being fully comfortable with my own body was certainly a factor, not knowing enough about myself along with not feeling confident enough to say anything when it was not working for me might've been another one. And, to put it plainly, sex confused me.

Think about it, sex is a very complicated thing. It can be very intimate and really meaningful one minute, and then be very casual, fun and light the next. It can mean so much, it can be powerful and beautiful with one person, but it can also be a drunken, probable mistake with another. It depends on the mood, the circumstances and the relationship with that person. So yeah, it is very conflicting. Especially in the first few years of discovering it. Sex can be a no-strings-attached situation but the catch is that nine times out of ten, strings do get attached at some point, for at least one of the two people having the sex. *I mean, they made a whole movie out of it!*

Because sex, whether you like it or not, is not a small thing. You're crossing that line with someone, you're letting yourself be vulnerable, in a way. Sure, you might have the occasional night of drunken sex with a guy or a girl you'll never see again, but usually, sex is an important thing. It can be great. It can be mind-blowing. It can also be a disaster. It's messy.

I don't think I fully enjoyed and appreciated how great sex could be until I was in my mid-twenties. I just wasn't understanding what everyone else was going on about. I think the misrepresentation in movies and TV shows didn't help. A couple having the most amazingly easy, happy-ending sex of all time in less than 60 seconds? People in school talk about how amazing sex is and how they can't get enough of it. How orgasms just happen every time a person has sex. And how, if you're in your twenties, you should be having a ton of mind-blowing sex. Excuse me, what?

It was everywhere. At the age of 21, I couldn't escape it and I just felt like I was missing something. Would sex ever be fantastic for me? And why wasn't it AMAZING every time I had it? At that age, I probably got more excited about an all-you-can-eat buffet than sex...*Who doesn't get excited about an all-you-can-eat? Too many puns here...*

So, with all those thoughts in mind, you can imagine how my feelings about sex became quite upsetting at times. When I was 23, I was with a guy for a few months. He was lovely, not one bad thing to say about him. We spent some great times together. And yet, when I think about him now, I just remember how much pressure I was putting on sex and how I didn't feel like I was ever going to be in a good place with it. I remember one time after we had had sex, I went downstairs and cried in my mum's arms. I cried because I didn't feel normal. I didn't understand why I wasn't enjoying it like everyone else seemed to be. What was wrong with me and my vagina? Why didn't it feel comfortable? Why couldn't I relax and enjoy it? What was I missing exactly? This also takes me back to the amount of time I spent worrying about what I looked like. Was I good at this? Did my body look OK? There was nothing relaxing, enjoyable or fun about it. Not then, at least.

If I could go back and have a chat with that girl, I would tell her to be patient and kind to herself. I would also let her know that she is not alone and that it does get better. Navigating your sexual awakening is part of growing up. The more you have sex, the more you'll discover what you like and don't like, and you will automatically develop more confidence and will feel more inclined to speak up when you want things done a certain way. I certainly have a much clearer understanding of what works for me now. It is obvious to me now that when I was in my early twenties, I didn't know myself enough and I didn't feel comfortable speaking up when it wasn't working or could've worked better. It takes building that confidence, that experience and knowing your body first in order to enjoy sex.

This does not mean it's always going to be unicorns and roses, my dears. Sex is a bit more complex than that. Confidence isn't present 100 percent of the time and our minds aren't always in sync with our vaginas. We all have off days where we're feeling a bit bloated or generally not feeling great about ourselves. It happens. But here's the thing. Whatever concerns you might have about your body at the time, I can promise you this: the other person does not care.

The guy or girl you're having sex with is NOT obsessing or caring about whatever concerns you might have about your body. They are having sex with you. They are probably over the freakin' moon to have someone naked in their bed! They are not thinking about your wobbly bits. If anything, they are probably thinking about their own shitty insecurities. They are probably more focused on what they are doing and what they look like.

So please, try and avoid getting too in your head about your body. Things just got a bit easier when I started letting go of all the things I was worried about when being naked with someone. Because, ultimately, they are naked with you too. They are vulnerable too. And if you still need some extra reassurance, here it is: they are having sex with YOU. Let's face it, they've already won. They are winning. Navigating that confidence is part of the journey. I'm not saying it's an easy one but it's tremendously helpful in order to start really enjoying sex.

Confidence will also come with knowing your body. Listen to it, explore it on your own and discover what feels right for you. Yes, I am talking about masturbation! It is one of the healthiest things you can do to boost your confidence, your sexual awakening and overall wellbeing. It just is. How can you expect to know everything about yourself, if you don't spend time down there exploring it yourself? If you haven't already, get cracking ladies! You'll be able to guide your partner, which will inevitably lead to better sex. *I also read an article once which said that masturbating makes you live longer...I'm choosing to believe it, don't take this away from me.*

So there's all of that. And also having a partner who listens, reassures you and knows what the hell they are doing in the sack.

I know it seems like a lot of boxes need to be ticked but it takes a combination of all these things for it to come together nicely. And then we're *really* talkin'. Navigating all of this is part of growing up.

The way I feel about sex now comes from a much more confident, freer, more comfortable place than when I was that 21-year-old crying about it. However, I am by no means an expert. Far from it. And it doesn't mean I'm not going to have bad sex again. This is not Disneyland. I probably will. *Although I don't think I'll ever let it get that shit again. I'm happy to report that my tolerance is much lower now and also when you're in love, sex is 100 percent better, no question about it.* But bad sex exists. It happens to us all. Nothing wrong with that, we've all been through it. That awkward, silent, painfully tragic sex. It's a nuisance for a minute and then we all move on.

A lot of pressure can come with sex but only if you let it. I think this idea that sex is going to be amazing all the time is a myth and a lie. I don't know who started spreading that idea around but it is not true. As women, the most important thing is to make sure we feel validated, listened to and confident enough to speak up when needed. The rest is sort of out of our hands. And rest assured, we have ALL had bad sex.

Here's the other 'entertaining' side of casual dating in London: the accumulation of hysterical, awkward sexual moments. I'm afraid it comes with the territory. My girlfriends and I have certainly collected a few gems over the years. *If you needed another reason as to why having girlfriends is vital in your life, this is a good one. You NEED to discuss this stuff with people to realise that everyone goes through awkward experiences.*

When you are single in a big city, it's kind of predictable that awkward sexual encounters are going to happen. My life has looked strikingly similar to Sex and the City at times. *Just without the killer New York apartments and insane clothes.*

I think when we hear 'awkward sexual encounters' we all have an experience that comes to mind. *If you don't, don't worry. I'm sure yours is just around the corner. Cue evil laugh.* I'm mostly talking about this because it's comforting to know that maybe you're not the only one that went through it, right? Because let's face it, there are so many things that could go wrong with casual dating and sex. In my circle of friends, it's mostly been a mix of this:

Guys who have no idea what they're doing, guys with micro penises, guys with humongous penises, guys who have so much hair you wonder if they're not actually a werewolf, guys who cum in 30 seconds, guys who take too bloody long to cum, guys who keep asking you if you've cum when they've just poked around for three seconds, guys who don't know where the clitoris is, guys who mistake which hole is which and guys who say weird shit during sex. The list is endless, and not a lot surprises my group of gals anymore. It is what it is, huh ladies?

What is quite annoying is that you never really know what you're going to get in the casual dating world and that makes having sex with someone for the first time a bit of a gamble every single time. So, if you are thinking that single life just seems like a walk in the park, think again. We are basically risking our lives, our sanity, and our poor vagina's health every single time, in hopes of having a decent shag. *There are many perks of being single, by the way. I'm just choosing to give you a specific side of it, in case you were thinking of leaving your boyfriend of five years because he leaves the toilet seat up every day. WE deal with Penis Freak Land and risk our vagina's health weekly.*

One thing that was very unexpected when it happened to me, a few years ago, was the fact that you don't even need anything to go wrong or be off-putting about the person for it not to go right. Sometimes you can have great chemistry when talking and kissing a guy, and then it just evaporates when the rub-a-dub-dub starts. It occasionally just doesn't gel and you can't really figure out why. The chemistry just vanishes. And that's a bit of a bummer for all parties involved because you actually become hopeful and quite confident in the fact it'll be a decent shag. *On the plus side, that's probably the least disappointing out of all of the options above. I'll take that situation over the guy who screams 'Yemen!' when he cums, or the guy who thinks your clit is one inch below its actual spot.*

So don't be too cocky. It can all go tits-up, even when the kissing is good.

Turns out, when this happened to me, it ended up being one of my most awkward moments to date. Take a seat.

I had gone on a handful of dates with this lovely Italian guy and it was going quite well. We hadn't slept together yet, so on the fourth date, I had chosen a bar that was close to my house. *Subtlety guys, wink wink.* We were talking about summer jobs and, somehow, my crepe-making days on the beach in France as a teenager were brought up. He said he'd really like us to make some crepes at mine tomorrow morning. *A little presumptuous of him to think he'd be staying the night but then again, he wasn't wrong. A girl gotta get laid.* I didn't think much of this comment until, all of sudden, after two cocktails, we ended up at the supermarket, grabbing all the ingredients to make crepes. I'm talkin' the whole shebang: flour, milk, eggs, even bloody Nutella and bananas. I wasn't really feeling the idea but he was excited. *Who was I to deprive this man of this random breakfast idea?*

We got to mine and my flatmate wasn't home, so he left his bag in the kitchen and we started fooling around. It was going OK, nothing amazing but nothing horrible either. Eventually, I asked him if he had a condom and he said 'Ah damn, they are in my bag, in the kitchen.' He was naked at that point. Since my flatmate wasn't home, I told him to go grab his bag. He left my room, and as he came back, the front door opened and my flatmate entered and was faced with this butt-naked human in the hallway. I heard the commotion and suddenly he jumped back into the room, fully embarrassed, and told me what happened. If I wasn't particularly excited before, this definitely was a mood killer. But the guy had embarrassed himself, dragged his bag into the room and proudly found a condom, I couldn't really shut him down. We then TRIED to have sex and it just did not go well. It was awkward, silent, and zero positions were working. I hit my head twice, he broke my new lamp and couldn't figure out what to do. The chemistry was... non-existent. After 15 minutes and two head concussions later, I gently told him 'Listen shall we just stop? Call it a night?' He was disappointed but quietly agreed.

Now, usually, this is part of the evening where I tell the guy to leave. Especially if the sex was average. I don't really like guys staying the night in the early stages of dating. Same, when I'm at their place. If I can escape, I will. *I'm sure a shrink would have a lot to say about this... I like the whole bed to myself and a full nine hours of sleep, OK? Sue me!*

Anyway, the night had been traumatic enough and it was 1 am. *I can be a bit of a bitch sometimes but I could not tell this poor guy to leave.* So, he stayed and I didn't sleep. He obviously slept like a baby. *I do not have the time or energy to go into how annoying it is that guys can fall asleep in 1.2 seconds. It just makes me angry and we have more awkwardness to get to.* So having slept about two hours, I got up at 8 am and dragged myself into my kitchen to find my flatmate with a huge smug smile on her face, asking for details. At that point, I was desperate for the guy to leave. I didn't want that awkward talk and I definitely didn't want another attempt at whatever sexual experience that had been. I just wanted him out. Fuck the crepes.

I became quite frantic and spent a solid 20 minutes trying to find any excuse I could give him to get him out of my flat. He was still fast asleep and it was 9 am on a Sunday. The ideas were limited. My flatmate, enjoying the situation too much, suggested I tell him I had forgotten I had a yoga class with a friend. I went back to my room and slowly poked him and weirdly whispered, 'HEY, excuuuse me, I'm so sorry but you have to go. I forgot I have a class with a friend and it's in 30 minutes.' The poor guy was so confused and sleepy. I made him a terrible coffee and we sat in silence in my room while he gathered his clothes and got dressed.

And then it got beyond awkward. I stood in the kitchen, waiting for him to tie his shoes and put his jacket on, while my flatmate was just soaking in every bit of the awkward scene. He came into the kitchen, still half asleep, and I don't really know what propelled me to do this but I grabbed the flour, eggs and Nutella and gave them all back to him. *I thought it was a nice gesture. Nutella ain't cheap!* He grabbed all the items in his arms and looked at me like I had hit my head on something... And because I didn't think I had made things ridiculous enough, I then carefully placed one of the bananas on top of the Nutella. I think my exact words were 'Here's a banana for the road.' So there he was, confused, holding a banana and a pot of Nutella while I was just apologising profusely about the fake yoga class I had forgotten about. My flatmate was staring at us like she was watching the most hilarious comedic sketch ever, desperately trying not to laugh. *It was a solid Judd Apatow scene if I do say so myself.*

I thanked him for a fun evening, closed the door after him and collapsed on the floor, wondering why life was so difficult. All in all, that evening inspired a few lessons: a few good dates don't mean one is immune to awkward sex. Always make sure they put their bags in the room. Book a therapy session if this particular situation ever happens to you, because let's face it, I definitely made that experience more awkward and dramatic than it should've been. And I should make more crepes at the flat. *We never spoke again after that but at least he had some Nutella to remember me by.*

That is the only sex story I'll allow myself to write in this book. If you ever meet me in person, maybe you'll get another, probably worse and less appropriate, story out of me. But my dignity still needs to remain intact for a bit longer.

Here's the good thing, though: sex can also be *effing* fantastic. *YES, I have had fantabulous sex guys, thank you.* It's true. Actually, really great sex is difficult to describe. Kind of like love. You just know when it's the good stuff. For me personally, being in love with someone elevates how great the sex is, in a major way, and how well you communicate with your partner is key. There is an intimacy that casual sex is not able to provide. This doesn't mean that you have to be in love to have great sex but it enhances everything because there is more meaning and connection there. When you're in love, there is a certain curiosity about each other. What the other person likes, what their fantasies are. It becomes a safe place, a place to explore each other's bodies. That's what making love is about.

Fucking someone and making love are two different things. That's something I found out when I fell in love. It's a different experience. It's caring, fun, passionate, respectful and very intimate. It's very multi-layered. Casual sex will be light, and usually single-layered. It's important to know that distinction.

So yes, great sex does exist, don't lose faith people! *And if you're one of those people who always has great sex and doesn't have a clue what I've been going on about, you can just sit down quietly, I don't think we're going to be friends...but good for you.*

What I would tell myself now, and for all of you reading, is that you'll go through many different experiences when it comes to sex. You'll have bad sex, good sex and amazing sex. You'll feel like shit walking home, knowing you probably should've stayed in that night. And you'll also have moments of feeling empowered, owning your sexuality, your pleasures and speaking out when necessary. It's all part of the journey. Sex will be odd, wonderful, beautiful, intimate, awkward, comforting, funny, fun and a major part of discovering yourself, physically and mentally.

I have to add, *contrary to what the hypochondriac in me obsessed over*, you will NOT get pregnant every time you have sex, or get some rare disease that no one's ever heard about because 'this article on WebMD seems worrying guys.' Just be safe and try to filter out the assholes. *Less risky when it comes to STDs.*

Finally, and most importantly, please don't think that because you're in your twenties, you are meant to be having sex all the time. That is a huge misconception. One that I am bursting right now. There were certainly times where I thought 'Oh gosh I haven't had sex in six months, and I don't really feel like having it but everyone else is. What's wrong with me? Should I not be wanting sex more often?' Everyone is different. Every person has different needs at different times of their lives. Don't compromise yourself when it comes to sex.

Ultimately, sex is much better when you are comfortable in yourself and feel empowered enough to know that you can say no and that it's a safe place to share your desires. YOU decide. Don't have sex if you don't want to and have sex if you want to. Do not do anything you don't want to do. Ever. Not one person should pressure you into having sex if you don't feel like it. I cannot stress this enough. This also means, don't ignore the red flags. They don't go away, they become bigger and bolder and more damaging. Always pay attention to how a person treats you and how they make you feel about yourself. If they make you feel less than who you are, walk away. You only deserve someone who listens and respects your boundaries. Nothing less than that.

I can't say I am particularly proud of every single dating moment I've had, but I have made a conscious choice to embrace the whole lot. They completed my twenties and filled that decade up with experience, lessons and great times. Through all the tragic dates, the failed relationships and awkward sexual moments, men have and still do teach me a lot about what I want and don't want. My standards are higher and clearer in my head and it took many dates, and many situations to get to this place.

In terms of being in a relationship, everyone has their own rhythm and priorities in life. Like I said at the beginning of this book, I've always been late to the party. To me, I fully believed that my twenties were not made to settle down and start a family. And for the few times I thought I should settle down with someone, because a few friends were doing just that, it didn't work for me because it wasn't meant to work. I was meant to keep learning because I still didn't know what I wanted. Your journey is just that; your OWN. Not only do you OWN it, but it is unique to you.

When you reach 30, more and more people will be settling down around you, and that's OK. It doesn't mean you have to do the same. You just do what feels compatible with who you are and that will be the right choice. No need to put pressure on yourself, every journey is different. And who knows, maybe by letting go of expectations, seeing what happens is when the right person comes along. *Just please let him be well-adjusted and ankle monitor-free.*

AUNTY ANGE TIPS

- Find ways to love yourself first before being in a relationship.

- Exes can sense when you're doing well, when you've just about started your healing journey, when you've moved on. Usually, this is when they pop back into your life. BOOM. Notification: 'How are you?'. They just have this radar. 'You're happy? Ok, I'm ready to shit all over it now'. If you are able to, don't let that happen. You moved on for a REASON.

- Be your own person outside the relationship you're in. Have your own friendships, your own activities, your own opinions. THIS IS VITAL.

- Never stop working on yourself, even when you're in a relationship.

- If you don't want to sleep with them, don't. No question about it.

- Avoid sleeping with someone at work unless you have a Plan B job offer.

- A first date should always be Drinks, in case you need a quick escape.

- Always hash out an escape plan with your friends before going on a date.

- Condoms are a drag but unless you want a baby in nine months or a potential STI, they MATTER. Big time.

- If you're planning on having loads of sex, having cranberry juice on standby in the fridge won't hurt...and lube, ladies.

- Not having sex for extended periods of time is not a big deal and definitely not something to obsess about.

- Nothing wrong with casual sex as long as it's safe and mutual. Don't judge yourself and don't let other people judge you.

- BOUNDARIES. Have them.

- Just because your best mate is getting married does not mean you have to settle with the first guy you see.

- Put your cynicism aside. *Yes YOU too, Ange*, and be open to love, it can be pretty effing fantastic with the right person.

Someone once told me: 'If it does not bring you an orgasm, inspiration or income, it does not belong in your life.' I think we can all agree on that one, right?

IV. WORK-LIFE:
BALANCING IT OUT

Work is ingrained in our lives from a very young age. We grow up seeing our parents go to work. We are constantly asked about our work – what we do, how it's going. Work is everywhere we look, in school, in life, in film, TV, music and books. It can be quite overwhelming. Not to be dramatic or anything, but work is something we're going to do, or meant to do, FOR THE REST OF OUR LIVES. *Ok fine, a bit dramatic.* It is a big deal though.

Regardless of whether you love your work or despise it, it's undeniably going to be a major part of your life – *unless you've inherited a fortune and enjoy sitting by the pool drinking a cocktail served by your butler all day long, you people can leave the chat... MAN, that sounds good right now. Ok, Ok I'm back in the room...* What I do for work isn't going to be the topic of conversation here. My relationship with work is what's going to be the main focus. Turns out, that relationship is important because it shapes how your life looks and how you feel about yourself in general.

In my twenties, I had zero clue how to balance it all out. My work took massive precedence over everything else because that's how I was going to prove to myself and to the world that I was worth something. A solid 80 percent of my life was dedicated to work, so my work became my life and when my work was crappy, I felt crappy about my life. My self-worth always took the hit. I'm sure you know what I'm talking about, right?

This chapter is one of the first ones I wrote for this book, mainly because I had kept a shamefully long list of ridiculous jobs I did in my twenties and I felt it needed to be shared with the world, in some capacity. Trust me, if you have any interest in finding out about the absurd side jobs an actor goes through in their lifetime, keep reading. And before you say that some of these jobs sound made up, I'm going to stop you right there. I would not make this stuff up for fun, I lived it. It's all true and aside from costing me my dignity, I like to think it's all pretty priceless. *Let's face it, my dignity was left behind in the Love chapter, wasn't it?*

Jokes aside, I spent most of my twenties consumed by work as I know a lot of other people are too. So, I really want to spend a bit of time focusing on how I managed to find my self-worth outside my work and look at how comparing your career and working situation to other people's never works, how standing up for myself, saying no when I want to and taking a stand at work was one of the most important lessons this aspect of my life offered me. Finally, I show how finding a work-life balance is truly key in becoming a healthier and happier person.

Your Work Does Not Define You

It's funny how most of us all go through a similar journey when it comes to work. We go to school, mostly in order to try to figure out what the hell we want to do or can do... FOR THE REST OF OUR LIVES. *There it is, that dramatic voice again, sorry!* We study and train for years in something that will hopefully appeal to us, FOR THE REST OF OUR LIVES. *I can't help it, guys.* We desperately hope that our idea sticks. Then, we seek out the perfect job. Even if that perfect job doesn't really add up fully in our heads yet. It's just what we are meant to do to feel good about ourselves, to have a purpose in this life, right? Or at least we tell ourselves that.

We then get a job. Great! It might not be the one we truly wanted but it'll do the trick for a few years until we figure out what we really want to do. We go to work every single day, seemingly content, finally on the right track, and feeling very 'adult'. And slowly, regardless of if we love the job or hate it, we begin to think that this is what identifies us as human beings. This is what measures our worth. This is what defines us in the world. I'm speaking generally, of course. *Some people have figured out that what you do for a living doesn't define you. Many have not. Myself included.*

This is not an obvious one to get perspective on. The concept of work has been with us for most of our lives. Think about it. As children, we are often asked what we want to *be* when we grow up, not what we want to *do*. The whole point of school is to decide what career we want and our teachers or parents are the first ones to put pressure on how well we're meant to do if we want to get the best job out there, which, convention says, equates to what kind of person we are. We are just used to associating our jobs with who we are. This means our self-worth is often measured by how our work life is going.

Our work is a major part of the entrance to adulthood. At first, it can be a scary, unknown, sometimes challenging place where we have to spend most of our days. It's unavoidable. We all have bills to pay! In addition to that, work gives us a sense of purpose on a day-to-day basis – or at least it appears to. But when you put all this emphasis on work, what do you do when it doesn't go well? When a pitch meeting falls flat? When a colleague is bullying you? Or when you realise you actually don't enjoy your work anymore? Well, usually, you take it out on yourself. You think you've failed, right? You think you're less of a person because it didn't work out or your job is beneath you, or you're not at the level you think you'd be at by now, or it simply SUCKS. And so, immediately, you think you're just not good enough. And then you spiral. 'Why don't I know what I want to do? Why am I not getting this job? Why am I not successful in my field yet? Am I not good enough? Why is everyone else around me killing it and I'm lost?'

How many of you mirror your self-worth to what you do for a living?

In our twenties, we put a tremendous amount of pressure on having to know what we want to do and finding a great job that will make us feel good about ourselves. Truth be told, many of us have no clue what the plan is at that age. I'm serious. We just don't. No one knows what they're doing! And that is more than OK. It's normal to feel lost, confused, frustrated or disoriented, and it's also completely OK to change your mind if you want to.

Maybe you thought you liked the path you chose at university but it turns out that you've finished a three-year degree and now hate the whole thing. Maybe you're seeing everyone else start building real careers and wonder why you can't find a job you enjoy. Or maybe you've just settled. Settled with the idea that perhaps you're not supposed to like your job. It's just a job, right? Either way, all these situations make you think that your self-worth has to do with where you're at in your career. And that is just wrong.

Let's face it, you can be a very successful lawyer and an absolute prick in life. *God knows we all know that soulless, corporate type, don't we?* You can be the best, most compassionate, smartest person – and be unemployed. What you do for a living does NOT define who you are as a person. It's a small part of your life, except it sometimes feels huge compared to the rest and if things go wrong at work it can make your self-esteem plummet to the ground.

I fully participated in this belief. My career was the single most important thing for me, a key component, especially in my early twenties. So much so that I let myself believe it was who I am and what I was worth – an all-consuming and fairly unhealthy feeling.

I knew I wanted to be an actor very young. I had big plans, big dreams, and set goals in mind. I am a very ambitious person by nature. It's a great quality to have but it can also be a curse. A curse because you can't decide to suddenly be 'un-ambitious', it's in your bones. It's a constant pursuit of something.

And it was in my bones, that's for sure. I moved to London with my head full of very ambitious aspirations. What *actually* happened during my first year went something along the lines of living in a house with seven people, from seven different countries, sharing my room with a very depressed Italian girl, *she had just had her heart broken,* waitressing at a pizza place where my colleagues hated me and getting auditions for low-paid short films and the occasional porn film offer from my agent. Think of Glamour and then think of the exact opposite of that and you're there. That was my life. I would love to be able to forget my first year in London, the year of eating cans of corn, noodles and cereal for dinner; it definitely humbled me right out the gate. It was a shock to the system and a realisation that this path was not going to be easy.

This rocky start did not slow me down. It did the exact opposite, actually. I became utterly *consumed* by plans and intentions. I was obsessed with getting to a certain level in my career by the time I was 25. *I think we all have that number in mind for some reason or another.* You can imagine my disappointment when things didn't go to plan and I still had not achieved all the goals I had in my head. Pretty much on a monthly basis, I felt like I was failing because I was not at the level I thought I'd be by that point. *OK, it was actually a weekly feeling.* And it just sucked. It was hard to shake the feeling off. It still is sometimes. Every single day is different and it's a tough ride. It can feel like I'm on cloud nine one minute and then I crash and burn the next. It's extremely unstable, which is probably why it took me so long to believe I was an adult.

On top of the harsh reality of not being at the level I wanted to be, I had, *and still have*, the constant rejection part of it. The amount of rejection is absurd. No normal person should have to go through it, frankly. *But what is it they say? Actors are crazy? Probably.* It's definitely not all unicorns and rainbows, I'll tell you that. And in that all-consuming way, it can lead you down a dangerous path. I don't really know why or how, but this idea that we are not worth enough because we haven't achieved our own standards or someone else's standards in the workplace is beyond me. What is up with that? That way of thinking is really damaging. Of course, work is important, but it is NOT everything and 2020 was an eye-opener for a lot of us.

We have all collectively been through a global pandemic. *I know, I'm trying not to mention the horror of it too much here, what a shit show that was.*

The world stopped and so did we. A lot of us were left without work and that raised a lot of questions about our identity outside work. We all had to look into ourselves and question what we truly were without it. And that triggered a huge amount of questions; not necessarily bad questions but questions that simply revealed who we were or who we aspired to be and what we wanted out of this life. Who are you without your job? Do you enjoy your job? Did you get it wrong? Did you get it right? What do you like outside work? Do you want to keep going the way you're going or is there something you haven't explored yet, at work or outside of it, that will fulfil you more? These pieces of ourselves would probably have been left undiscovered without that pause.

I definitely felt like a huge shift was necessary in how I viewed my work at that point.

When the world stopped, the film industry did as well, which meant I stopped. And I was VERY confused and overwhelmed with this feeling called Who The Fuck Are You Now Without Work? It wasn't fun.

When you're an actor, you're either working or looking for work; it's a full-time job. And it's very easy to get into the mental habit of thinking 'Oh if I'm not working, I'm not worth as much as that other actor who's booking all the jobs' or 'If I haven't done a TV role by this age, I'm worth nothing.' It became my form of identity. I fully believed that what I did for a living, the number of jobs I booked and didn't book, equated to who I was as a person. I was consumed by it to the point where I didn't know who I was outside of the business. So, when work stopped, I had to seriously ask myself who I was outside work. What exactly does this all mean? Who am I meant to be now? Is there maybe more to me and to life than acting? It just raised a huge amount of identity questions. Important ones.

I live in the city and we all know city people are driven by work and building a name for themselves in their careers. And that's great! It's a wonderful goal to have. But there might be such a thing as being 'too ambitious.' Is it possible that work can take a bigger place in your life than it should? I guess it depends on what your purpose is and if you've discovered that part of yourself yet.

I love my job. I wouldn't trade it for anything else. But it is a brutal, relentless, tiring job. The ups and downs never stop. Therefore, my view of it needed to change because it became too painful. I reached a breaking point not long before the pandemic. I couldn't hear another rejection. The 'It just hurts a bit too much' from Emma Stone's *La La Land* scene is pretty much how I felt. The pandemic forced me to take myself out of the game. I disconnected from the constant hustle that had become part of my daily life.

What people need to know about the acting life is that when actors are not on set working, they are not sitting around doing nothing. We are looking for work, auditioning, doing side jobs, and applying for jobs. It never stops. It's relentless. So I stopped. I couldn't really recognise who I was because all I thought about was acting or hustling to try to get the next job. I didn't know who I was anymore outside that life. And that got a bit scary. So I said *Fuck This*, I want to see if I can be an actual person outside my work for a minute and see what it's like to have a life outside that world. And most importantly, learn to love me without the pressure of work in the back of my mind.

And let me tell you, it didn't even take two days of waking up and not having to look at my emails or job applications to get my breath back. I could finally breathe. My head already felt a bit clearer and lighter. I was paying more attention to the people around me but also to how I was feeling about myself. I ended up learning so much about myself during that time. Asking myself the right questions. This was a choice I had made – to force myself to stop and take a breather. The funny thing is, once you let go of whatever is blocking you at work, good things actually start happening at work because you've focused your energy on your life and your wellbeing. The tables have turned, and your work is now defined by you and the new energy you bring to it.

It took a global pandemic for me to realise that there might be more to me than what I did for a living. Isn't that BONKERS? As with so many people, the world needed to stop to make me stop and appreciate everything I had in my life and my own self when I wasn't chasing a casting. Turns out, there *is* a life beyond being an actor! I can be a whole person without having to scan my emails for jobs, send off that casting tape, book that role or write that script. I can enjoy life and discover more of it outside my work.

How did it take me 29 years to realise I didn't need an acting job to prove I was a great human being, full of talent and qualities? I had to take my head out of the game for a bit to be able to breathe and find myself again. The pandemic, with its lockdowns and furloughs, as daunting and scary as they were, did make it possible to look into our lives and decide what we wanted to fill them up with. Some people took up online Zumba classes, others got into 'paint by numbers' and realised they loved painting. I bought a guitar and actually learned how to play. I started to draw, I saw my friends way more *after the lockdown ended OF COURSE*. I meditated and discovered yoga. I booked trips I had been putting off. *I'd like to say I took on cooking but I don't want to lie to you, guys. My cooking is still horrendous.* I explored a whole new me, outside of work, and it felt glorious! That period in time made me realise that it is possible to have that work-life balance if we actually focus on the things that make us happy and fulfilled.

It's not easy. Work starts up again and then what do you do? Well, you can choose to put a chunk of time in the week for yourself and for what makes you happy. Even if it's just in the little moments. Making a living and supporting yourself is obviously very important but what is equally crucial is taking time for yourself. There is a way to balance it all out by prioritising certain times for passions, hobbies and loved ones, while also working. It's dedicating your life to yourself and making sure work doesn't take over everything else.

Turns out that limiting myself to my job was absurd. There was no reason why I couldn't combine it all.

You can thrive in your work. You can be amazing at it and honestly, that's awesome. Pat yourself on the back. You've found your path and if you feel great about it, that's all you can wish for. What I'm saying is, there has to be a balance. You can't let work define you. It should actually be the opposite. *You* should define your work. And you'll be better at it when you figure out who you are outside it. What does that person look like?

I'm also here to tell you that no amount of stress is worth it when it comes to work. I realise this is a very easy thing to say because we are often put in stressful work situations. But unless you're a doctor or a pilot, *and a bunch of other super important jobs I don't have time to name*, no one will actually die from things going wrong at work. The stress of it will never be worth it affecting your life. Work cannot have that power over you.

When I think about my mid-twenties, I think of all the hard work, the agony of waiting to hear from castings, and the stress I put myself through in trying to be the best and achieving something before a certain age. It makes me exhausted even just thinking about it. I don't think it's how I am meant to live my life. It's quite unfulfilling and clouds so many other beautiful things I have in my life.

One of the big lessons I learned along the way is that sometimes things are just not going to go the way you wanted them to. For various reasons. My mistake was to try and force things that weren't supposed to happen at that time. If I didn't get a part in a film, if I didn't get a callback, if I wasn't getting any work, if things weren't happening when or how I wanted them to, I would beat myself up about it and it made my self-esteem drop and my negativity levels spike. And that is not appealing to anyone. There was a sense of desperation there. I was pitying myself, making myself a victim and starting to doubt my worth because work was not coming in. Suddenly, I was questioning life decisions. 'Had I made the wrong choice by moving to London? What was I thinking, I'm not supposed to be an actress? This was a stupid idea, I'm stupid.' The line between who I was and what my work was suddenly intertwined and I got completely lost. Ultimately, this had to happen for me to shake this problem off. It became important to take a step back and realise that maybe I didn't get that role because I wasn't ready for it when someone else was. What is meant for you won't pass you by. It's about trusting the timing of your life.

This is why it is key to have a semblance of a life outside of work. If not, you're going to realise, after 20 years of going to work every day, sunk in an endless routine, that you haven't lived at all. You haven't seen the world. You haven't explored what you are outside of paying the bills. To me, having been consumed by work for most of my twenties, that thought terrified me. It's really scary to realise that hobbies didn't exist, that trips were few and far between, that I hadn't seen some friends in a really long time. And the work consumption had created this dark hole for me to sit in, alone. And if I was having a bad work week, I would feel like a disappointment, like a failure. It's damaging and that kind of thinking can't go on forever.

I completely understand and am fully aware that for many people, working is not only about ambition, it's about survival. It is not an easy world. I can only hope that most people can find a balance and find glimpses of happiness outside of work. I do believe that there is more to life than work, no matter how important the job is to you or how much you want to succeed. If you don't try and build a balance, you might lose yourself in the work.

Just think of it this way: When you're 70, going down memory lane, are you going to remember that awful client meeting where nothing went according to plan or are you going to remember that holiday you took where you hooked up with that gorgeous lifeguard? *Fictional, of course...* PERSPECTIVE. The pandemic was awful. No doubt about it. But what it gave many of us is perspective.

You can still be amazing at your job, you could have the best job ever and people respect you and praise you but at the end of the day, what brings you joy and happiness? Work can make you happy but work alone can't just be it. What about everything else? Finding happiness in so many other things, big or small. Isn't it by being a daughter, a mother, a friend, a sibling, a human being on this earth? Is it by travelling, seeing the world? Or even a good home-cooked meal? *Or if you're like me, a greasy takeaway.* Can you honestly tell me that your work, every day, brings you peace and fulfilment? Is it worth all the attention and anguish you might be experiencing because of it?

These questions can be overwhelming because, at the end of the day, we all have to work, right? We all have bills to pay and shit to buy to survive on a day-to-day basis. My point is simply to observe how much of your life is consumed by work and is it worth it? Is there maybe a way for you to balance it out with a life outside of work and most importantly, not letting yourself be defined by it? I don't have answers to all these questions, at all. But I do have a broader perspective than when I was 25, thinking I was worth nothing because I couldn't book an acting job that month. I definitely see some progress. And I hope you have that bigger perspective too. If you don't, then read this again. Become your own person and decide that your work, as great as it might be, is just a job. It is NOT who you are. You are more than what you do for a living. You might be doing amazingly, you might be on that seventh unemployed check, it won't make you a better or lesser person because of what you do for a living. I am more than acting. This perspective gives me a great sense of relief. And funnily enough, the minute I let go of that belief, more jobs and opportunities came my way, and my work found me.

It is wonderful to have a job you love, no doubt about it. But what defines you is everything else in your life. Your friends, your family, your experiences, your memories. Compassion, empathy, openness, kindness. Those things matter more.

Focus On Your Own Path and Take Risks

I don't know who needs to hear this, but it is OK to not know what the next step for you is. If you're unsure what to do next, if you're unsure about your choice of career, if you feel lost in what job you want, if you need a minute, take that minute. Everyone has their own path, their own story. It certainly does not mean you're less of a person because you haven't figured that part of your life out yet.

One of my closest friends turned 32 last year. She's been at the same job for eight years, and has recently realised not only does she not like her work anymore but she is also thinking about potentially going back to school to learn a new set of skills in a new field. She is extremely hesitant about it because of her age and she wonders if she should maybe just suck it up and continue in the line of work she's in. 'It would just be easier to stay where I am,' she says. 'Going back to school, surrounded by people younger than me, it's depressing.' On the contrary! It's now or never, isn't it? The alternative is staying in a job that makes her miserable. At 32 years old. No thanks. *Don't worry, I gave her a kick in the butt and she's applied to do a one-year course in a few months. Quietly proud of myself for that.* My point is, try not to be too hard on yourself. You are allowed to take more time in your choices of career if you need it. No need to panic if you don't know yet or if you change your mind along the way. It happens, more times than most!

And if you want a change of career at 30, 40 or 50, so be it. It's your life, you can do whatever you want with it! And if one of your excuses is that it's not what most people do, well, who cares? When has comparing yourself to other people ever helped? I mean, listen, I'm not saying that in my weak and dark times, if I'm having an especially hard week with work, and I need a bit more of a kick in the face, I don't check social media to see what other actors I know are doing and filming that week, which obviously makes me feel like a complete utter failure. I'm HUMAN. Of course, I do it. We all do it!

Especially artists. And yet, it really accomplishes NOTHING.

Unsurprisingly, it isn't the best feeling in the world when we see someone working on an amazing job, in an exotic location, looking so happy in Barbados or wherever. *I'm being a tad too specific here, I might have to rein it in.* Ugh, it's the worst. It doesn't help your self-esteem and it doesn't help the situation you're in either. You just end up feeling twice as shit.

There are always going to be moments when we think everyone seems to know what they are doing in all aspects of their life. Looking at their Instagram pages, they seem to have it all figured out, right? That's what we do, we compare ourselves. That's the dark side of social media, isn't it? We can check what everyone else is doing, all the bloody time, 24/7, and see all these seemingly great and fulfilled lives. Then we spiral.

So, when I had finally had enough of feeling crappy about myself looking at other people's accomplishments, especially during the worst weeks of my career, I decided to really look into what was causing this unhealthy feeling. The main thing I realised was that social media wasn't serving me in a good way. I wasn't using that tool in a healthy, productive way anymore. I was scrolling endlessly through people's lives, in quite a numbing way. So, as I mentioned previously, in order to alleviate these insecurities and freak-outs, I deleted social media for a few months. It was pretty radical. And for those few months, it really helped me refocus and regroup. There were no distractions. After a few months, I did reinstall it on my phone but with amended terms; I unfollowed or muted accounts that had a negative impact on my mood and I capped my usage daily intake. Setting those boundaries for myself was key for my mental health and the way I felt about myself and my work life. Not having the constant reminder that people were killing it at life every day, seeing their fabulous lives on display every day, was helpful. Small thing, but it didn't hurt.

On top of managing my social media usage, here's something that I like to remind myself from time to time: Social media is a LIE. One day, an actress came up to me and said: 'Oh Ange, I follow you on social media and, my gosh, what an amazing life you have, it's inspiring to watch. You seem so busy and working all the time.' I thought she was joking, but no. According to her, my life on social media looks like I have a dream life. The irony. Especially as I had spent most of that week crying over failed castings and lack of work.

So please, stop comparing yourself to everyone around you. Trust me, we're all just blabbing our way through it all. I can guarantee you that everyone is going through some sort of shit. No one really has a clue AND social media is to PROMOTE the good stuff. No one's going to share that photo of them eating on the floor of their living room, crying over something. No. It's filled with happy pictures that probably don't even show 10 percent of what's actually going on.

Everyone has their own journey and what I've realised is that we have no idea what is going on in someone else's head: most of the time they are dealing with their own demons. We all are. So, stop that. Focus on being you, doing the work, doing your best and growing in your journey.

Growing in your journey can also be done by documenting your progress; writing down all the little things you are doing every day to keep afloat. It's a great way to assess how much you are putting into yourself and your happiness. It's also a great way to be grateful for all those little steps, nothing is too small. I would also say that setting goals or intentions for the week, or month, is a good motivator. Obviously, don't beat yourself up if those goals don't happen! I'm not saying it's a set-in-stone list but it might give you a better focus and intention for the time ahead. A clearer path. Overall, try not be too hard on yourself. Just make sure you keep focusing on your own path.

Speaking of focusing on your own path, this will be especially important when taking risks in your career and might come into play when people around you have opinions about it. Taking risks in one's work, and in life in general, is exciting and scary. But mostly exciting. It's easy to play it safe and be complacent. There is nothing wrong with that – if it suits you. But you need to be aware that this element of comfort might hold you back from making progress. Now, maybe you're at a point in your life where comfort and safety are just what's needed; it's what you want and you don't want anything else than what you have. Fucking wonderful, you've made it.

For others, there might come a point where taking risks is needed: You know you should move on because you are not challenged at work anymore, you feel bored, you feel too comfortable, you've learned everything you needed to learn etc. Or maybe you should go for that job you've always wanted before it's too late, or maybe it's time you speak up about this particular issue before it becomes a permanent situation.

Try not to be afraid of taking risks. Especially if it's related to what you should be doing compared to what others around you are doing or what they are saying to you. People will always have opinions. What matters is how much you let that impact your decisions, when it comes to your own career.

When my dad turned 33, he left his very well-paid job, with its many perks, to build a business he truly believed in, from scratch. And he did this regardless of what his parents and friends thought he should do. How terrifying and amazing is that? It takes a lot of guts and faith in yourself to do that. Leaving a job, when you have a family to feed and where financial security and comfort are at the forefront, seems impossible. And yet, what do you do if you want to feel challenged again, if you want to feel that you can contribute to the world in a better, more fulfilling way? You take that leap. You just do. Because the alternative is years in that exact same place, wondering what could've been if you had taken the risk 20 years ago. Let's not forget that wonderful quote, by Jim Carrey: *"You can fail doing something you hate, so why not fail doing something you love."*

I certainly applied this philosophy when I decided to move to London and be an actor. It's super scary but was it going to keep me in quiet, safe Brittany all my life? No. I took another risk when I tried to make it in Los Angeles for a while. That didn't work out, so I came back to London and survived that experience. I took another big risk when I changed agents in London.

I had found out my acting agent was submitting me for only French roles. I am French, yes. But I'm also British. Applying for French-only jobs meant that I was missing out on 80 percent of the other jobs, which, to me, made zero sense. But I was finally with a reputable agent and I didn't want to risk him firing me over me doubting his agenda.

Months went by and I was chatting to one of my friends in acting class and she told me there was a great role in a period drama I would be great for. I told my agent and he said it was a British role. And that's when I felt I needed to say something. I knew that if I didn't speak up, it would've never left my mind. Regardless of what he might do, this was my career and I knew I was perfect for the part. I wanted to be considered for the casting. I told him that and he said he didn't think I'd be called in but that he would submit me for it anyway. The next day I got called in for the casting and I was recalled twice for it. I didn't get the job, but the casting director later booked me for another English role in that show. Two months later, I decided to drop my agent and go with someone who I felt could recognise my full potential. My 19-year-old self would never have even thought of doing that. I would have agreed with this big agent, rationalised with the fact that I was inexperienced and probably didn't know what I was capable of, and never got that casting. Twenty-nine-year-old me KNEW what she was capable of and was not going to back down without a fight.

This doesn't mean that you should go with every instinct you have, of course. But when it comes to taking risks, you have to know if it's worth fighting for. If the answer is yes, then take that leap of faith, and do it for yourself. That's where progress comes from.

David Bowie once said:

"If you feel safe in the area you're working in, you're not working in the right area. Always go a little further into the water than you feel you're capable of being in. Go a little bit out of your depth and when you feel that your feet aren't quite touching the bottom you're just about in the right place to do something exciting."

In our twenties, we usually think we have to play it safe. We have to follow the rules. Maybe we have to follow what our parents are doing and saying. Well, I'm here to tell you that you don't. You have to listen to yourself and if you have an idea, an inkling that maybe you need to change your path, do it. And don't wait for the right time. There isn't going to be one. Just pick a day, pick a moment and jump. Be fearless. See what happens. *And you better come back to me with a full report.*

Not every risk taken is going to be a success. There will be failures, probably many of them. But you are doing your very best, we all are. You're being brave by attempting it. And when things aren't working out, when that risk didn't pan out the way you wanted it to, there is usually a reason. Maybe it's because it's guiding you towards something better. Maybe you were supposed to learn something there. Keep following your own journey, regardless of what other people's careers and lives look like. You will get there, at your own pace, in your own way.

Insight On The In-Between Acting Jobs

Aside from being on set and actually getting paid to act, booking any sort of work in the acting business is a full-time job on its own. It's a big, consuming job that doesn't pay any bills. You can spend days, weeks, even months chasing roles, going to castings, harassing your agents and screaming into a pillow. I knew that this industry was tough and I was fully prepared for the challenge. What hadn't occurred to me, however, was the ridiculous amount of 'in-between' side jobs I would have, the ones where absolutely no use of acting was involved. *Well, if you call pretending to give a crap about the job in question 'acting', then maybe a bit of acting was involved, yes...* I promise you, if there was ever a prize for 'CV with the most ridiculous jobs ever', I'd win. No question about it. *It's not an Oscar but I'd bloody bring that hard-earned prize home and proudly put it on display.*

Just sit back and let me entertain you with a mix of some of the wackiest side jobs I've ever done, going from the ridiculous to the really absurd. Here we go. *Now, when I say ridiculous, I don't mean stupid. It is not my goal to offend anyone here. No job is stupid. I mean 'ridiculous', in the sense that I was either not qualified for that particular line of work or the job didn't feel like an actual job. When we get to the pink flamingo toy fiasco, ridiculous does actually mean RIDICULOUS, though. Enjoy.*

Let's start things off with the category I like to call: I Can't Believe This Is How I'm Paying My Rent Right Now.

In third place:

The one where I was a Bag Search security guard at a very famous Royal Palace. *Yes, you read that correctly.* A promotional agency I used to work for, whose jobs usually involved giving out gift bags at events or holding a shitty 'Exit Here' sign right by an exit door, hired four of us to work at Kensington Palace to be actual security. Bear in mind that most of the people on this agency's books are artists, musicians, actors, writers or students. We accept these jobs in high hopes to very quickly move on and do what we all came to London to do. We don't do these jobs as real careers. We want to do a good enough job to keep being hired until we get an acting gig. We do not take them seriously. However, bag search security felt like a bit of a drastic and fairly concerning leap, very far away from the fluffy world of useless promo jobs.

This was a situation where we *actually* had to deal with people's bags in search of potential weapons, before they entered a pretty prestigious royal building. I will never forget the first day on this job. We had a briefing with actual REAL trained security guards and I just remember all four of us loonies, looking at each other with utter confusion, when we realised what we were *actually* here to do. We were so used to coming to work and pretending to be useful for a few hours, while trying to take as many breaks as possible until the day ended. This particular situation felt wrong and absurdly funny at the same time. I remember one of the bodyguards saying 'Don't worry, it's pretty rare to find anything sharp in these bags. These tourists aren't really the knife-carrying kind of people,' as he laughed away.

None of us were trained on what to do if a weapon was *actually* found in one of these bags, by the way. We just went along with it, hopeful that we wouldn't encounter serial killers attending the Diana exhibition.

So there we were, two of us on each side of the entrance, 'looking the part', all dressed in black suits, *although the girl next to me was this tiny blond girl who looked like Tinkerbell and no amount of suiting her up would make her look threatening in any way,* wearing latex gloves, rummaging through stranger's bags. I distinctly remember the first time I asked someone if they had anything sharp in their bag and really thought 'How is this my life? Where did it all go wrong for me?' Four actors just making a living.

What was fascinating was getting a proper insight into people's lives and bags. Personally, after a while, the job went beyond looking for anything that could potentially kill us. I got invested in finding out something odd or unusual in these people's lives. *Give me something to go on, some sort of gossip while I pretend I'm a trained security gal, you know.* Well, let me tell you. People's bags tell us EVERYTHING we need to know.

You can bet that any lady over 50 will have some sort of caramel hard candy in their bag and will 100 percent offer you one. *I started to get offended when they didn't.* Every dude, especially if with a girlfriend, would have a very nervous look on his face the entire time. Every girl under 25 usually has every makeup product under the sun in there, which meant my gloves were going to get covered in powder, foundation or a red lipstick gone rogue in the bag.

And then we get to the weird folk. I had a sweet-looking lady once, who came in with two kids and had a full-on kitchen KNIFE, the size of my head, in her bag, next to the kids' homemade snacks. Her face did not flinch when I pulled it out. I nervously looked up at the *real* security guard for help. We had to confiscate that one and she didn't give a clear indication as to why she was carrying such a humongous knife in the middle of the day in Central London... Quietly moving on from that one.

Another memorable one involved the most innocent-looking old lady, around 70 years old, coming with her gal pals to visit the Diana exhibition. Before I looked in her bag, she pulled me closer to her, leaned over and whispered: 'You might find some unusual things in there my dear, I'm staying at my boyfriend's house tonight.' And right on cue, as I was rummaging through her bag, I saw a bright purple vibrator and some risqué underwear. I looked up at her, smiled and said, 'Good for you Ma'am, and also, thank god I am wearing gloves.' Good times.

I could go on and on about that job; it was many things, but it was never boring. People will never cease to surprise me and I hope they never stop.

Eventually, after six months, the job was taken over by real security people and us actors had to go back to finding other weird-ass jobs.

In second place, we have the Flan In a Van job.

Again, this was sold to me as an ordinary promotional job for this new flan coming out. *Who the fuck still eats flan, I do not know, that's beside the point.* The job was simple. Myself and another girl would drive around London with a shed-ton of different flavoured flans and try to get as many grocery stores in London as possible to take a box and see how many get sold in a couple of weeks. After those few weeks, we would come back to every store we did and see how many were sold. Seems like a pretty easy gig, right?

Well, a few things went sideways very quickly. First day on the job, we find out we're not driving a car, we're driving a big-ass VAN through London, with a fridge big enough to carry a thousand flan pots. *Thank god the Aussie chick I was working with volunteered to drive it. I can't even drive a car. Let alone a ridiculously large van.* We then find out that we have to FILL UP this fridge van with flan every morning at 6:30 am. AND we have to HAND-PICK what stores we were going to visit that day, write them down on a sheet and head to every single one of them on that list every day. One of us then had to go in and try to convince the managers to take this shitty flan and have it on their shelves for a couple of weeks.

Think about this for a second. This is London we're talking about. Do you know how many convenience stores there are in this city? A shit-ton. It would've taken us most of our twenties to get through it. Oh, and the client didn't want us to go to the big stores, so we had to go to the tiny, dodgy-looking ones. You know the ones you go in to buy gum and try not to touch anything else? Yeah, those ones. Also, do you know anyone who even likes flan, to begin with? I certainly don't. Try convincing run-down convenient stores in North London, that barely sell normal yoghurt, to give flans a try... Zero chance.

Luckily, they had hired two fairly resourceful gals for the job. We may not have given a crap about flan but we definitely wanted to get the job done and over with. We got creative with it. Thankfully, there was a limited amount of flan to give out every week. So, along with us both, sitting in this van, in the corner of Piccadilly Circus, eating a yearly intake of flan every week, we did have tricks up our sleeves in order to get rid of it very quickly. When I say tricks, I mostly mean bending the rules a little... which involved giving four boxes per store, instead of just the one we were meant to give out or stopping by our friends' flats and giving some for them to try...and their friends. *Which makes me think I could've hosted a killer flan-themed party at my house. Opportunity missed there.* Or stopping for coffee in cute cafes along the way, getting them for free in exchange for 'a yummy protein flan.'

Listen, I'm not saying we were the BEST employees ever... but you can commend our boldness. All these surely sackable ruses meant we were done by 10:30 am every day. *Is it really necessary to be driving in a van all day when one can easily get rid of 500 flan pots in three hours?* The client evidently didn't think the entire job through... The job where we worked two hours a day for two months. They were just happy we were getting rid of so much flan every week. Come to think of it, I think we even got a bonus for that job.

I will never eat flan again in my life and there were definitely *'what the hell am I doing with my life moments'*, but, in the absurdity of it all, we did have fun driving around, listening to music, and sitting in the park. I learned that trying to sell flan to people wasn't my career path but it surely improved my selling tactics because, believe it or not, those flans did end up in their bloody fridges.

Oh and if you're wondering, the flan company went bust, everyone hated it and we all went back to our lives after two months. Good times.

Finally... are you ready? *I'm not sure you are...* The one with the Pooping Flamingo.

The mother of worst jobs so far goes to the time I worked at the Toy Fair, a three-day event in London. Sounds fun, in theory. I remember agreeing to it thinking I'd be comfortably seated behind some sort of welcome desk, maybe greeting the guests, giving some guides and potentially getting some free toys for my niece and cousins. *To be honest, with my job track record, I really should've expected the kind of loony job that this turned out to be. I should have predicted lunacy. But I like to be optimistic, and I expected this to be just a normal job for once.*

Well, guys, I didn't get a desk, not even a chair, actually. I was put on a stand where I had to demonstrate a toy to potential international buyers. I did not KNOW what toy I'd be showing, nor did I have any knowledge of toys in general. I basically was not aware of anything that this job entailed, which was not my finest move, I'll give you that.

So, I walked in that morning not having a clue what I was going to do for three days. The boss explained the job as we walked to the stand. The second he said I was going to be at a stand trying to sell toys, disappointment started to settle in. Not only was I not going to be sitting at a desk, eating my snacks and looking at my phone all day, this meant I was going to have to *talk* to people and engage with them on the subject of toys. Not my jam. But hey, so far, I could live. It was acceptable. I would get over it. *You're probably thinking, gosh this woman is lazy... and you'd be correct!*

We got to the stand and this is when the boss tells me that I'm really lucky. The toy I'm demonstrating is brand new, it's really funny and there's quite a lot of buzz around it already. This is when I look at the stand and see 'The Pooping Flamingo' in big pink sparkling letters, next to which was a pink fluffy flamingo sitting on a toilet, crapping some sort of glittery orange sand, while dancing and singing 'Uh oh, I gotta go, I really gotta go'. All. day.

Long.

I do not have enough *time* to explain to you the sheer pain of this moment. I like to think I am a good actress but there was not enough talent in me to hide my shock and disgust about this. At that moment, I really thought my life had become the universe's absolute number one goal of Let's See How Ridiculous Ange's Life Can Be. And it had. Scraping off the orange glitter sand from the toilet every time the flamingo crapped was not the highlight of my life. What was worse is that obviously everyone found out about this pooping toy, and it was the most popular thing at the fucking show. And I had to DEMONSTRATE how it worked, every time. I have no idea how I lasted the three days without punching someone. It definitely involved a lot of wine to forget it had happened. If there was ever a 'What the hell am I doing with my life' moment, that was it.

The job really did ruin flamingos for me, though. The species is dead to me now.

There certainly have been many jobs that really shouldn't be called jobs. From dealing with a guest list in the parking garage of an event, scanning people in and out of a conference room, being in charge of giving a microphone to people at a medical conference, where a Q&A never happened – *quick tip, if you're a hypochondriac, don't work somewhere where you're going to hear all the things that could kill you. Not ideal* – leading a team of 10 people through a London shopping centre for the promotion of a new baby pushchair, pushing EMPTY prams around for hours, *which really freaked people out*, giving away free t-shirts to people to promote a new dating app that never came out, and doing market research for a mattress company that ended with me sleeping in one of the store beds because not one person entered the store that day. I think it's safe to say my CV is up there in Most Eclectic and Random Resume Ever.

Being an actor is so much more than being on stage, on TV or on the big screen. It's a lifestyle. If you haven't figured it out already, actors are generally pretty good at pretending to know what the hell they're doing and what they are talking about. We're hustlers, we're resourceful. We've got endless tricks up our sleeves and are prepared to use them all if it gets the job done. And I used them all. I like to think that, through the years and the many different absurd jobs, I've learned a lot. Some pieces of information will without a doubt be completely useless to me in life; like that time I worked at the Defence terrorism show where I had to promote shields and how to wear them. *Very light and fun show, as you can imagine.* Or when I sold wellington boots at the Chelsea Flower Show where I had to learn about all the different shapes, perks and materials a boot can have to protect your feet from any weather known to man. I surprised myself with how much of an absolute pro I became selling water features at the Ideal Home Show. I was selling them like hot cakes on a cold day. People were buying these ludicrous, ugly water features like their life depended on them because I made them believe they needed this fashionable dolphin fountain with an extra light installation, a solar option and a high-temperature feature for their garden. Frankly, I have surprised myself with all the information I've been able to retain with each job. Whether it will serve me in life or not, *emphasis on the not*, somehow, I blagged my way through it all without a hitch. *Let's face it, pretty much none of these will serve me in my everyday life. The only thing working at the Allergy Show gave me, was the depressing image of how many allergies a human can have and it's fucking terrifying. My life's a breeze compared to the guy allergic to butter and love.*

This lifestyle has taught me how to think on my feet and it has opened my life up to many different jobs and interests people have in general. It's a big world out there! I have joked about most of these jobs but truthfully they have taught me how to be patient, open-minded, curious, and interested in other people's ways of living or jobs. I've met a lot of different people from all areas of life and everyone is just trying to make their own business, company or job work for them. I might not be very interested in the actual product or line of work, but it doesn't mean I haven't enjoyed the jobs. I've made the most out of unusual situations.

And I've certainly had a laugh. Writing this chapter has made me realise how few serious jobs I've had so far, aside from the real acting jobs. This might be why it's taken me this long to feel like an adult. Just look at those jobs! It's utterly ridiculous how anyone could expect me to feel adult-like after that. Pooping Flamingo guys, *a pooping flamingo.*

When I look back at it all, I just laugh because that's all I can do. I didn't take them seriously and I think that's why I had fun and remember them fondly. Most of all, aside from the wackos I inevitably encountered during those jobs, I met some of my best friends during some of them, and that is the best gift I could've asked for from these experiences. *On top of it making a really funny chapter for you guys to read, of course.*

Preserving Your Integrity In the Workplace

Throughout our twenties, we're mostly spending time finding our feet in the workplace. We have a lot to learn and the stakes can feel quite high. We want to impress, climb the ladder and achieve goals by a certain age. However, when you're an inexperienced 20-something, people can take advantage of you and make you feel like you need to jump through a thousand difficult hoops to get to a place where you can make demands. Of course, we all need to learn the ropes of the business we choose and that means doing the grunt work and paying our dues in some ways. However, this does not mean you are a doormat. This does not mean you have to be silent if something feels off. Realising that I had a voice and that I was entitled to use it, was something I learned over time. Or maybe I knew I had a voice, I just didn't feel like I was in any position to use it.

When you enter the workplace, you enter it with new, fresh, enthusiastic and naive eyes. You go in, full of ambition and motivation. You don't necessarily think about the obstacles along the way that might challenge your self-esteem and confidence.

The fact is, people are going to try to take advantage of you in some way, at any point in your life. I wish I had known that, so I could've at least prepared myself for it without feeling like crap.

My first job in London was waitressing in an Italian restaurant. I had just moved from a small village to The Big City. I was motivated and excited. I was thrilled to have some sort of job that would keep me going while I go to castings. But I was naive. Waitressing is a difficult job at the best of times. Add a few staff members who are all siblings and hate your guts, then we have what I used to call Hell. Anywhere from giving me the hardest tables, to lying to me about sharing the tips when I should've kept my own. *And I'm a nice gal, I actually WOULD get the most tips from the tables out of all of us and yet, they led me to believe all the tips had to be shared.* This went on for three or four months before it came to one particular night, where I snapped. I had endured a lot of mockery, jealousy and just plain rudeness for that period of time and one night, I was holding four very hot pizzas in my hands, walking up from the kitchen to the restaurant floor, beyond exhausted by the hours and the fact this was my seventh shift that week. My hands were shaking and the staff were just enjoying the scene. I got to the final step up the stairs and that's when I tripped. All four pizzas went flying in the air like I was in a freakin' cartoon movie, and one of the pizzas slid under a couple's table. Before I had time to say anything, the gentleman stepped his foot into it. The roaring laughter of the restaurant broke and the staff started to applaud while I slowly got up, mortified. I looked around the restaurant and stopped at the staff, grinning their faces off. I slowly took my apron off and threw it over to them. I think my words went something along the lines of Fuck off, I quit. In my state of fury, or possible delusion, I remember grabbing a slice of pizza from one of the plates and walking out while eating it. *Pretty badass image, isn't it?*

No one should have to endure any kind of bullying at work. Period. It is never justified, no matter how high up the person is. It can be a tricky one to navigate but with age and experience, we do, hopefully, learn what kind of crap we are not willing to take anymore and what we deserve. The twenties are there to develop some sort of voice for yourself. Sure, it might get pretty rocky. I think it's supposed to be. If it was smooth sailing at work all the time, I'd be concerned. We all encounter people who either don't believe in us or don't like our way of working and we have all dealt with the crappy boss or the annoying colleague from time to time. That's kind of normal, it's to be expected. Everyone has a different way of working, a different voice. There are going to be conflicts. However, there is a difference between conflict and disrespect. One can be constructive, the other is destructive. When the latter occurs, things can get a bit messy. Your self-worth is challenged and how you deal with it will improve over time. The more confident you feel about yourself and your work and the more experience you gain, the more you'll know how to face these hurdles head-on and stand up for what you think is right.

You have to have your own back. You have to be your own cheerleader because some people will try to put you down; it's just how some people are. Not everyone is going to have your best interest at heart, especially when it comes to Work. The workplace can be a loving, supportive environment but it can also attract competition, jealousy, narcissism and abuse of power. How we deal with those challenges is a massive learning curve. We've all heard of or had that colleague who gives someone a hard time for no reason. When unwanted negativity kicks in, you are fully entitled to use that voice and be heard. Put your foot down. No one should make you feel less than you deserve, remember? You have to be able to stand up for yourself, even if it's SUPER scary. And believe me, most of the time it is terrifying. But if it feels right for you, then I promise it'll pay off.

I am a very different person now than when I first moved to London. That naive, innocent, confident, inexperienced young girl could not have even fathomed what she was going to experience in the next decade. It does build a thicker skin, though, and eventually, you know your worth.

Knowing your worth can be recognised in various ways. A lot of the time, 'Show me the money' is a good starting point. And there is absolutely nothing wrong with asking for more money when you know you deserve it and that you've earned it. The only catch is that you need to be prepared to potentially lose the job if it backfires. There is always an element of risk to the game, which is why I always say ask for what you feel will make you feel valued, listened to and happy with the job, and then have a backup plan if the answer is no.

More often than not, when you ask for a raise or a higher rate for a particular job, you need to feel confident enough to back yourself by showing proof of your experience but also how valuable you are to the person and the job in question. You need to be able to not be replaceable. You need leverage. And if you don't have what is necessary to show that yet, work harder in order to make sure you have leverage and that you are worth it when the time comes to ask for that particular position or raise. This obviously takes time and experience. So please don't be too hard on yourself. Your only job is to be the best you can be in your field and people will see that and eventually will match your efforts to the money or position offered.

My brother, the pastry chef-model dude, had been working at his pastry job for nearly four years. He was tirelessly running the kitchen, with a team of five people. His hours were insane, but he knew he was irreplaceable in that kitchen. He was the most intuitive and the most creative chef they had. He was also the youngest manager there and the most talented one. *And no I'm not biassed, just try his chocolate eclairs and you'll know what I mean.* After three-and-a-half years, he knew he deserved a raise. His creations were selling like hot cakes and for a 26-year-old, already in charge of a team of people, all older than him, he was in a position to make demands. And so he did. He asked for a significant raise very confidently because he was also prepared to walk away from the job if the money didn't meet his expectations. There was no fear, just proof that he was worth more. In his case, it worked out. *Three months of negotiations later though... Some bosses really like a fight.*

It takes a lot of courage and confidence to reach a place of demanding more for oneself. However, I've learned that, in order to progress and feel satisfied with where you are at or where you are heading in your career, taking a risk is a major part of the game.

For me, it was a change in my standards that made me raise the bar for myself.

When you start out in the acting business, people tell you it's about getting as much experience on set as possible, regardless of the quality of pay. You have to start somewhere, right? It's about building a CV through experience. In the beginning, that's mainly gained through student films, little corporate gigs, short films and profit-share plays. This means that for the first few months up to a year, you are working on very low-budget projects. It's just the name of the game. When you're a young actor, you just want to be surrounded by actors, doing what you love. And frankly, I wouldn't take any of it back. Getting national minimum wage for a lead role in a short film when I was 19 was an awesome experience. I learned a lot and got an agent from that footage. I was getting paid pennies but I was inexperienced, doing what I love and someone was paying me something. It was great. But very little money to actually live on. *Hence the traumatic side gigs.*

But there came a time when that had to stop when I needed to figure out what I deserved. I needed to draw a line in the sand as to what jobs and what rate of pay felt acceptable for me to take on and what I was going to decline, once my CV got stronger. It took me years to feel confident enough and experienced enough to ask for a specific rate of pay and make sure that number wouldn't budge. Standards have to be raised for you to feel like you're progressing, to feel like you are doing better work. It's a natural progression. It's about setting a bar for yourself. And I did.

I mentally made a note of a number that I was going to start asking for acting jobs and made a decision that I wouldn't take less than that amount anymore. I had the experience, I had the credits and I had progressed in my work enough to do that for myself. *By the way, I'm not talking about a huge number here. But it's just nice to have an amount in your mind and try to stick to it.*

I started asking for that amount and it didn't always work. There have been times when I've lost, *which is usually when something better has come along.* Some companies like to take advantage and offer tiny amounts of money to actors who WILL say yes because they really need the money. I've been there. But I have also won many negotiations where production companies have agreed to pay what I asked for. There's no better feeling than that feeling of validation, people agreeing to your standards. It's empowering, it's satisfying and is a huge boost to your self-worth. You just have to confidently lay down the facts. If you have experience, if you have a particular set of skills, *enter Liam Neeson's voice here,* and if you feel that you can bring something unique to the table, if you have HOURS of tireless evenings working on a project under your belt, if you have leverage, then trust that what you are asking is right. Again, confidence can win over the most sceptical. You have to trust that you're worth the rate and if they pass, that's too bad. Something else will come along and most of the time, it will be something better.

I'm not saying I haven't strayed from it. *A girl gotta eat!* Of course, I sometimes needed to outweigh the risk by demanding more, and figure out my needs at the time. Do I need the money right now? Or can I let this one slide and hope for something better?

There were times when I had to decide if I was going to stand up for myself or suck it up, and take the money, because that month, rent was more important than pride. I've definitely accepted jobs for ridiculously low money and even though it doesn't feel good, I also know that at times, it was necessary.

Those moments are few and far between nowadays. I'm no longer scared of asking for what I think I deserve or simply saying no to jobs that I'm not comfortable with. And that doesn't mean I won't lose jobs. I definitely have. I can't tell you how many times I've lost jobs after asking for a little more money to meet my male co-star's salary. It's the name of the game. There are risks. But there are also times when I've asked and they've agreed. How rewarding those moments are. Knowing you explained why you are worth more and confidently, respectfully make your case... and actually win! Pretty badass, if you ask me.

I am obviously talking about quite a specific industry. Sometimes, people can't give more. Sometimes there is no room for progress in the line of work you are in. And that is absolutely valid if you are content with your situation. But if you think you are worth more, why not try to do something about it and push through when people are reluctant to give you more.

A very interesting thing that I've noticed is that if I ask for a bit more money on a project and the client tells me they don't have the budget for that, this is not always the truth. Numerous times, the next day, once I've passed on the job, they'll get back to me and miraculously will have found more money to pay me. *Funny how that works, huh?* You simply have to weigh the risk versus the reward and go from there.

Knowing your worth isn't about how much money you're making though. Everyone has a different amount they are satisfied with. Acknowledging your worth in the workplace comes from not accepting anything less than what you feel comfortable with. If you are forced into something, if a particular situation makes you uncomfortable, if someone makes you feel disrespected, this is where you need to stand up for yourself. Set some boundaries for yourself. Take a stand. Draw some lines. Be your own support system. This is just TOO important.

I heard the actress Elizabeth Olsen say in an interview once: *"NO is a full sentence."* I LOVE that. It's simple. Not only can you say no if it doesn't feel right to you, but you don't always need to give it an explanation. No means no. You don't want to do this and you do not have to. You don't need to expand. You can just say no. This obviously applies to all areas of life but work is a good example for me since I had to learn that maybe, in the acting industry, not every job is one I should take. Maybe if the job makes me feel uncomfortable, undervalued, or diminishes me, maybe it's not a good idea to say yes just because your team is pressuring you.

There is nothing more important than your integrity. Preserving it is first and foremost. Please don't ever do anything you are going to wake up to the next morning, look in the mirror, and not feel good about. If it means saying no to the big dogs, so be it. There is always another gig, always another chance somewhere else.

Saying no is a big one in my industry, especially since most of the time you can't afford to decline a job. But as you get older, you realise that how you feel about yourself will matter more than that paycheck. And if you know that particular job, or working with that person, or that situation, is going to affect you negatively, I genuinely don't think it's worth the money. You have to make yourself a priority. Your mental health and self-worth are at stake.

If you feel you are not being valued enough in your line of work, or at your workplace, and you can do something about it, do it. You can. And people will respect you more for it and it'll lead to bigger and better opportunities.

Two of my best friends have amazing jobs right now. They worked their butts off and have both acquired a tremendous place in their companies. They are valued and respected there. It's been pretty inspiring to watch. *Don't tell them, though, I won't hear the end of it.* But they did not get there easily and the hours they work at their jobs is mind-boggling! To the point where I've had to sometimes mention: 'Hey, maybe working 80 hours a week when you're being paid for 40 isn't such a great idea...' And even in very respectable positions, they have struggled to ask for some leniency. It's not an easy task when you know a lot of people rely on you, but I am here to say again: you HAVE to make yourself a priority. There is no use working yourself under the wire for a job. It'll be damaging and affect your life and who you are way too much. Eventually, one of them did ask to hire someone to delegate some of her workloads. *I like to think my advice and nagging her over her insane hours had something to do with it but she'll never admit it.* Saying no to working overtime is NORMAL. Why on earth are there so many people working more hours than they are paid for? I don't understand it. Do you not like your life outside of work? Are you trying to escape your life by not having one? OK, OK, I may be harsh here. Some people just can't get enough of their work and that's amazing. They want to work as much as possible and they feel validated there. As long as you are happy with that, then I will be happy for you. But if you are feeling run down, overused at work, or under too much pressure for you to handle, that's when I feel you are entitled to take a step back and find a solution there. Learn to say No. Put your foot down when you need to. Limits and boundaries are key to a healthy, working life and you will feel so much more content and validated if your worth is heard.

I can't tell you what to do in life, I can barely tell myself. But I can tell you that speaking up, standing up for myself and figuring out my worth in the workplace has served me more and played a tremendous role in shaping who I am as an actor and businesswoman. Your self-worth, and keeping your integrity intact, are what are going to matter in the long run.

Sure, it's never really an easy path. We deal with rejection, fallbacks, pay cuts etc it can be brutal... And if it's sometimes too difficult, try to surround yourself with people who are going to cheer you on, even when you're not in the mood to cheer yourself on. Do not let anyone tell you that you can't do whatever you set your mind to. You are your own person. Now go do what you're meant to do! *And if you have a boss who's a nightmare, it usually means they aren't getting laid enough, feel sorry for them. Just a thought.*

AUNTY ANGE TIPS

- No is a full sentence. I'm using this one again here, it's just too good.

- Taking risks is necessary to evolve in your career. Big or small, nothing is too little to matter and move things forward. Try putting that fear aside for a minute and see what happens.

- Not every risk is going to work out. It's OK. Grab some chocolate, some wine, or a friend, the next thing is just around the corner. Congrats on taking a chance! Keep going!

- If someone at work is abusing their power, making you feel unworthy or treating you in a way that makes you feel diminished, speak up. Nowadays, there is a very good chance you'll be heard and people won't let that linger. And if somehow you lose that battle, then you're better off leaving that space. Nothing is worth sacrificing your well-being.

- If you're not doing a job you love, I would suggest you find something else on the side that you love doing to compensate for the weight of that job. Make life fun outside work. Painting? Singing? Playing the guitar? Make sure to find time for a hobby you enjoy.

- Maintaining a work-life balance can seem impossible at times. Don't be hard on yourself. We all go through it. The sign you're working too much is when your friends or family tell you they haven't seen or heard from you in a while. That's a good wake-up call.

- Find your happiness outside work. As an actor, that's a super tough one and I still work on it every day. But moments of happiness are not meant to be solely from work. And that's what we all should work on.

- When you're struggling to make a decision about work or a career move, a pros and cons list is always a valid option.

- In order to make a tough decision, what I also do is imagine how I would feel if I said 'yes' to something and then I do the same if I had said 'no'. How do those 'pretend' decisions make me feel? That's my answer.

- Choosing your career path can change over the course of your life. Make sure you choose a path that fulfils YOU, not the person next to you. Make lists of things you want to do and achieve. Write down goals, and things in life that make you happy, big or small, and that path, your path will become clearer as you grow and progress in your life.

Do NOT worry if you haven't figured everything out when it comes to what career to choose. No one knows what the hell they are doing, EVEN when they find the right job for them! So, just take it easy on yourself. It WILL work out.

V. FAMILY & FRIENDSHIPS

No family is perfect. *Isn't that just the understatement of the year?* But it is quite a useful thing to know – in case you thought your family was the most screwed up and unusual on the planet. Rest assured, they are not.

Family isn't meant to be perfect. It's a combination of intense messiness, unlimited contradictions, unconditional love, incredible support, insane conflict, uniqueness, tragedy, hilarity, destruction, disappointment and unapologetic complexity. *Did I get that about right?* Family is also a bond, whether you want to admit it or not. It doesn't have to be a great bond, but you and the members of your family are all bonded in some way, shape or form.

Regardless of how your relationship might be with your family, it's undeniable that you can learn a lot from them, through the good and the bad: the misunderstandings, the disappointments, the divorces, the laughs, the fights, the disastrous family holidays, the hilarious birthdays, the drunken Christmases... Every single family really does have their own complexities. And that is fascinating to me. Because, whether we like it or not, they do have quite a bit of influence on how we decide to live our lives. There is something quite universal about that.

Being influenced by your family doesn't mean you're *going* to live how they choose to, of course. Sometimes it can be quite the opposite. You might find yourself observing some family members, and think to yourself 'Oh I *definitely* don't want to be like that, I do not understand this person.' Those observations and experiences shape you.

It's about choosing to take or leave bits from our family members' characters and ways of living and turning them into something you can call your own. I like to think that you can learn from every single member of your family. Even in the trickiest of relationships, at least you can decide what you're NOT going to do when you grow up. It's certainly what I tried to do.

Some relationships are just going to be more complicated than others and that's when the real lessons stand out. Others are filled with more unconditional love you could've hoped for. Family: it is a beautiful thing.

In this chapter, I am going to talk about navigating family dynamics; how it's not always smooth-sailing finding your place in that group and also how you can find your way in a world outside of how you were brought up. I'm going to talk about expectations, seeking validation from your family, realising that no family member truly knows how to master life and discovering that actually, everyone is just doing the best they can with what they've got.

Aside from the family you're born into, the one you don't *actually* choose, there is also – if you're lucky –the family you get to build and choose to have every day: your friends.

In my twenties, I spent a lot of time figuring out who my true friends were – in other words, pinpointing the signs that maybe not every seemingly nice person along the way was going to be a friend. I consider my friends now to be my family, but I had to filter a lot of the crowd along the way and that was done by paying attention to the signs. The only way to recognise the signs is to go through them and live them. Friends are going to be such pillars in your life, simply because these people shape you into the person you are today or will one day become. It was really eye-opening writing this chapter and discovering all the ways they can shape us. It's also obvious: true friends will be the only ones you can truly rely on and that will be a lifesaver at many times in your life, but particularly in the messiness of your twenties. Especially female friendships. I cannot speak highly enough about the bond women can have. We definitely are going to be delving into how vital women supporting women in this world is. Life pillars, never to be taken for granted.

Navigating Family Dynamics and Finding Your Place

There is something really bonkers to me about the fact that we are born into a family and we all grow up in the same household, 24/7. It is odd when you think about it. Why do we end up amongst this particular group of people? A group that can sometimes not be compatible. We're basically a mash-up of very different personalities living in a house for many years, spending holidays and social gatherings together. Aside from living under the same roof and, most of the time, sharing the same blood, the amount of stuff we have in common is pretty limited. When you think about it, it's quite bizarre. However, it doesn't mean there won't be tons of fun and hilarity! There is something quite powerful and special about it. Families are complicated and sometimes it's tricky to navigate the various personalities that create one family and where to find your place in it. It is a process to find your footing, your voice within the family, and outside of it.

I consider myself unbelievably blessed when it comes to my family. *I mean, sure, they are a bit wack but what family isn't?* They are wonderful, loud, flawed, inspiring, messy, beautiful people. From the crazy road trips, camping experiences and skiing holidays to simply cooking with my grandmother, playing Nintendo with my brother and laughing hysterically with mum about nothing, it's been a ride! I had a wonderful childhood; I was lucky. However, that doesn't mean it was a walk and a laugh in the park when I entered my teens and twenties. In my early twenties, especially, that's really when I started to realise that how you are brought up as a child, and what you're going to remember, will have an impact on your later years. There have definitely been times when I've felt a bit like an outsider and moments where I have had to use my voice a bit louder in order to be heard and understood in the way I wanted.

To understand this, it's important that I describe my experience in my family and how I've navigated through it so far. I need to preface this by saying that I had an amazing, privileged childhood and what I'm about to say does not take any of that away – *you hear that family?!* We will figure out how to find your place in the family through the hurdles and differences but also how a family's view of who you are, and what you stand for, should not get in the way of your happiness.

I grew up in two countries, England and France, with a family on each side of the pond. Two families that could not have been more polar opposites. The English side is upper middle class, conservative, and lives in Oxford. The French side is a working-class, small-town, liberal family, living in Brittany.

The English side is quite traditional, extremely kindhearted and generous but isn't really prone to speaking about any sort of uncomfortable feeling or emotion they might be having. Conversations were never that intimate, as if there was a line not to be crossed. It was deemed inappropriate and not very welcomed at the dinner table. *Brushing things under the rug*, as they would say. I was the first granddaughter on that side of the family and that came with quite a lot of expectation and pressure. I was polite and perfect, to a fault. There was no room for error. *Or at least that's how it felt.* From the ages of 5 to 12 years old, I had to ask permission to leave the table and not forget my napkin on my lap. That seemed to be what was expected of me. When you're a child, you don't really think there's anything unusual with this. You don't know any better. You don't question it.

I always had to dress immaculately when seeing my grandparents. *If you look at photos of me that young you'd think I was a royal child. Everything was bows and velvet patterned dresses.* I learnt the piano because it was considered posh and it meant I could play for my grandparents. I was bilingual at five years old, and as much as I understand that it was something they were very proud of and wanted to share with everyone, there was an element of being a show-off child to some. When I became a teenager, this expectation of being perfect lingered. I really felt the pressure of having to be GREAT. I had to be very good in school in order to get a GREAT job. The main questions I remember being asked by them involved my grades, how my piano lessons were going – *the lessons I absolutely hated* – and what I would end up doing for a living. It was pretty much constant, on a loop.

Don't get me wrong; the time I spent in my grandparents' house was absolutely lovely. So many joyful moments. I learned how to bake with my grandmother, she taught me how to sew and how to save money, and she was definitely a huge influence on how I conduct myself when I want to be heard and stand my ground. She was very protective of me, and I could feel that. However, the first grandchild syndrome never really went away because I felt that anything I did would not be good enough. I couldn't be messy in that house. And even though I wanted to read books, watch movies, buy flashy clothes, travel the world and do theatre, I never wanted to disappoint my grandmother. So I did catch myself putting on a heightened version of myself when I was with her – trying a bit too hard for her and my grandfather to like me and find me as endearing and as smart as possible.

One summer, I stayed at my grandparents' house for a month because I got a summer job in a creperie van in Oxford. Again, along with trying to save money for my acting school, I think I was also trying to impress them. Show them that I could work and hustle. I just wanted some sort of validation. Which is, when I look back, entirely backwards. This was my family and I should've felt comfortable enough to be messy, outspoken and myself, completely. *Sadly, I realised recently that this 'seeking validation' doesn't really go away that easily. Keep reading.*

You can imagine the reaction I got when I told them that I was going to move to London to be an actor. The silence in the room was very loud. My grandmother never stopped supporting me, though. I like to think that deep down, she admired me for taking such a clear original path rather than the teacher/journalist route that was expected of me. As for my grandfather, I still wonder if he really likes the idea...

When my grandmother got sick and sadly passed away, it left a big hole in that side of the family. Things weren't really the same after she left. I still try to maintain a relationship with my grandfather, with a few visits and phone calls here and there. It was not always easy. He is the sweetest man and means no harm, I know that. However, there were a few burns he unknowingly and clumsily caused along the way. A few years ago, he wrote his annual 'end of year' letter to the neighbourhood and recapped the whole year and what everyone in the family had been up to. Guess who was not even mentioned in the letter? Yep, velvety-bow dress little me. I actually pushed that one very far down inside for me not to focus on it too much. I keep trying to reassure myself that there was not much to read into that one...*let me call my therapist real quick though.*

Overall, once my cousins became teenagers and I no longer had to be the perfect teenage grandchild, it sort of enabled me to wash my hands clean of whatever I was going to do. The focus had shifted, and I was free. A little forgotten, sure, but free. It wasn't easy but I didn't want to dwell on something I couldn't control.

Nowadays, whenever I go see my grandfather, I still feel quite antsy. I am very happy every time I go see him but I always find myself being on edge right before - unfortunately preparing myself for any upsetting comment towards me or my career that would undeniably ruin my day. There is no real ease there. I still feel like I have to put on a perfect persona for him. I guess that little six-year-old girl, forced to sit up straight, speak in a posh way, napkin in lap, feels that it should always be the case in that house, even as an adult. And I hope, deep down, he is proud of me for choosing my career path and going with my gut. The only shame is that it is very unlikely it will ever be said out loud.

Navigating all of that wasn't always pleasant. Not feeling like I could completely be my relaxed self never went away but I found out that finding my place in that side of the family was actually going to happen outside that environment. I could only hope that they would look at my life from afar and be proud. Trying to impress my grandfather hadn't really worked but I did learn that seeking validation from your family isn't something you should strive for in order to be happy. Seeking approval, recognition and support is sort of out of your control. You have to find a way to be happy and fulfilled with your choices, regardless of what family members think. I definitely ended up embracing being a little different from that side of the family and if that meant not being completely understood by them, I learned to accept that.

As an adult, with all the perspective and life experience you gain, there is certainly room to reignite relationships with family members that weren't very prominent growing up, and appreciate the bond just as it is. Those small chats with my grandfather now, mean everything. They are precious moments. I found this also with my aunt quite recently. I have much admiration for her and how she conducts her life. She is such a beautiful person. Very cool gal. We are both so happy to see each other when we do and that is enough. Sometimes, it is just about recognising how precious those moments are, without them having to happen often. In that sense, finding your place in the family can be in the short but happy moments you share with them.

My French side is very much the opposite, meaning, it's *all* feelings and emotions. A lot is put on the table, amongst a lot of women, which doesn't come without its complications. It can certainly be chaotic. Family dinners: I wouldn't be able to tell you where the napkins end up, but certainly not calmly on my lap. You can bet on these dinners being loud, messy, opinionated, angry, tearful, everyone trying to get a word in, laughing until we pee, then angry again. I wasn't the first granddaughter, so the pressure of being perfect and wiser beyond my years wasn't felt as much – pretty much not at all, actually. The outspoken, ambitious and flawed me was definitely encouraged more than anything in that house.

However, I also had to adjust and get used to being around strong, opinionated women. When you go through puberty surrounded by beautiful French women in the family, it does create some insecurities about yourself. I had such admiration for my cousin and my aunt. They were both so cool, so beautiful and so completely themselves – unashamed, untamed. They worked in a club, went out with the hottest guys, and had this magical social life that looked amazing. I admired them and wanted to be like them, without ever thinking I could.

French culture had a huge impact on how we lived our lives day-to-day. It was basically all about food, drink, laughs, group gatherings, then food and drink again! I did spend most of my teenage years in France, so obviously that brought us closer than the English side, who we ended up seeing less often. However, amongst the many fun camping holidays, the French aperitifs, the hysterical road trips, the ski trips, the Christmases and New Year's Eves we experienced, there had been quite a lot of pain endured. And there was no hiding it. It was unapologetic, it was real. My aunts and cousins went through a lot and being a witness to how beautifully they handled themselves and went through some really tough times, was very inspiring. They didn't always get along and there were arguments but at the end of the day, they showed me how strong family bonds can be. The philosophy was clear: be human, make mistakes, forgive and move on together. It felt ok to be flawed and reassured me that I would still be OK. They made me want to be as strong, independent and as myself as I could possibly be because they were not shy to be themselves and live their lives according to who they wanted to be.

I don't think most of that side of the family knows how much of an impact they had on me. They are too humble for that. My cousin decided to become a photographer when she was 18 and she went for it, all in. She really believed in her talent, and she excelled. Without her knowing, she was a huge influence on why I thought I could take a leap of faith in my career choice. She made me believe I could do it. My aunt was a bartender in a club and when I was old enough to go out, she made sure she was as protective of me as could be. I always really felt protected in her presence and that has, since then, been our dynamic, that I cherish so much. And don't even get me started on my grandmother. *She has a whole feature later in this chapter.*

Overall, this messy group of women helped me find myself and let me be myself. I like to think I found my place in that family by just being who I was, by making bold choices and being as brave as they are.

What I'm trying to say is most of the time, family dynamics are messy. You won't always be understood the way you want them to. Hopefully, what you get is acceptance. However, if you don't, please try not to spend too much time trying to get recognition, approval or even support. Sometimes, it just won't happen. But what you can do is try to hold on to some core family members, find your voice within your family and create some great memories in the process.

What is remarkable, though, is that my view of my family is completely different now from how I saw them as a child and a teenager. I've discovered that they are all flawed, and they are all navigating the ups and downs that life puts us through, trying their best, just as I am. This is why they have taught me more than they could even know. If you don't think your family has given you some lessons along the way, look again. I promise you, they did. You don't have to like the idea, but you can be grateful for it. Let's talk about it.

Families: They Are Not Perfect But You Can Learn From Them

When I was nine years old, my dad took me and my brother to the cinema. When we came home, my mum told me to take my brother and go watch TV while 'mummy and daddy have a chat upstairs.' Instantly, I knew something was up. Mum never told us to watch TV if she could help it. We usually get told off watching too much of it! So what was going on? I did as I was told and I sat my brother down in front of a cartoon. Suddenly, I heard screaming, shouting and the throwing of objects. I turned the TV up and waited. Something was wrong, very wrong. This was unusual. My parents never fought. I had never seen them have one single argument since I was born.

Half an hour went by and my dad came back down with a suitcase and a pretty distressed look on his face. He didn't say much. He just gave us both a hug and said we would see him soon. I went upstairs to find Mum crying, cleaning up the smashed picture frames of their wedding and a cracked laptop on the floor. That was the day I discovered my parents weren't the perfect couple I had been a witness to so far. They weren't two untouchable, invincible heroes who had the answers to everything and knew everything.

Whether we like to admit it to ourselves or not, our families play a key part in shaping who we are. They just have this huge impact and that's why observing them, listening and learning from them can only help you become your own person. Learning from family members comes from watching them and seeing how they live, seeing if that's something that fits your personality, your wants and your goals in life.

We usually discover how flawed family members are when we start becoming adults ourselves. As we grow older, we become more aware of them and when this happens, we slowly discover that they are far from perfect. And that's when the fun begins. That's when reassurance kicks in. Indeed, no one *actually* has a clue what they're doing. It's a pretty insane and confusing moment, wouldn't you say? When you realise your parents aren't the picture-perfect humans you grew up to think they were. It's golden.

Everyone is flawed, even your mum and dad! It's such a crazy realisation and kind of heart-warming. Finally, there is some level ground here. The bubble is burst. Your parents aren't these magical creatures that seem to know the answers to everything and fix every problem. You will witness them screwing up. They will get aggravated, impatient, clumsy, drunk or angry. They will be WRONG from time to time. Isn't that nice? It kind of evens the playfield a little. Therefore, the opportunity to learn is huge. It really does allow us to learn from them and their mistakes, as well as what they can learn from us.

I was the first child, the eldest, which meant, to some degree, I got the wrong end of the stick. I was the experiment child. My parents were 27 years old when they had me and had to learn as they went. My mum has always said she was born to be a mother and there is no doubt about it. My dad, on the other hand, would make no such statement. At that age, he didn't really know what he was doing and I'm sure that was very overwhelming. Unfortunately, this made our relationship quite tricky to develop in a good way when growing up. *Something he has definitely admitted to me since having more children.* I simply wasn't lucky in being the first kid. Not to say he wasn't there when I was a kid! No, no! He was present for the cute moments, for the Polly Pocket play dates, for the dance rehearsals and for my first ever theatre production. *Which was bloody dreadful, bless anyone who was in that audience.* He filmed me with his old camera everywhere I went, he made funny bits to make me laugh and he danced in supermarket aisles to embarrass me. I have many great memories. But he also didn't know how to be there in a way that was helpful to me, he didn't know how to be strict without being frightening, he didn't know how to talk to me when I wasn't OK and he didn't know how to be supportive without being demanding of success. He had a lot of growing to do before being able to do that.

I only really paid attention to this when I entered my twenties and our relationship was still not great. My dad was going through some personal problems and somehow, as the eldest child, I was the one having to try to fix him and be there for him. *Or at least I thought I had to be the one to help.* All the while him not being there for me. We were both living and working in London but London life was taking a toll on us both, him more than me, I would say. That's when I started to become a witness to how lost my dad was. The reality is, our parents also have moments of being just as lost and confused by life as we are. I certainly remember seeing those moments in my dad and being constantly really surprised that he did not have his shit together. I won't go into details, *mostly because I still want him to love me after this book,* but the moments involved alcohol and a dingy club in

London. I'll let you imagine that story.

Truth is, some moments fractured our relationship for some time. As a first child, there is a certain expectation to achieve great things; there is pressure. Whether my dad realised it or not, I had put a tremendous amount of pressure on myself to make him proud and yet, I rarely got any recognition for what I had achieved or awareness of what he had put me through in my early twenties. Those chats never really happened.

It even came to a point where, after I had helped him organise a work event for the launch of a product he had created, *which went very smoothly and successfully might I add*, the night ended with him telling me the whole thing had failed and that I was a disappointment. We didn't speak for nearly a year after that event. I had been trying so hard to get some kind of validation from him by putting the work in, for his own business. Not only didn't I get any of that recognition, but I had also been shot down by deeply hurtful comments in a long and awful email he had written to me the next day. I had had enough of not feeling like I was enough as his child. Especially compared to his other four children who could do no wrong. I think somewhere down the line, he had forgotten that I was his child, not his colleague, partner or buddy. I was exhausted and gave up on even trying to be in his life. After nearly a year, he reached out and we managed to talk things through. I hadn't really moved on from how I was feeling but I decided that I could at least forgive him for the hurtful comments he had shot my way.

Surprisingly, it didn't mean that I suddenly stopped seeking some sort of validation from him there and then. I didn't even realise I was doing it and yet, every lunch we had, every coffee catch-up was filled with me trying to embellish every moment of my life and left me feeling like I hadn't achieved much or that I simply wasn't enough. And I couldn't figure out why I left those chats feeling this way.

So, the years went by, and somehow I was still seeking validation from someone who had not only not been very present but had put me through some really shitty moments in my early twenties. This went on for *years*. Up until last year when I realised that I was still seeking some sort of validation from my father. That feeling hadn't really gone away. Trying to get something out of him that would finally show me that what I was doing for a living and who I was, was enough. The thing is, I knew I would never completely get this validation. I think it might be in the way he grew up. His parents weren't prone to giving compliments, or obvious support, out loud. It might not be in his nature.

From my experience, I just get comments from my dad, banter if you will. Comments I would brush off, avoid, ignore or simply accept. It's how our relationship has always been. It felt kind of harmless. I didn't know anything else. It became such a habit that I couldn't even see he was doing it anymore. Until the day I brought my boyfriend to meet my dad at his house for the first time and he completely called me out on it. On the way home, in the car, he told me he didn't understand how I could laugh off those dismissing comments about me and my work. I was shocked. I didn't even realise how much I was doing that until he pointed it out. Once I realised this, I went through all Dad's comments from the past day and I couldn't believe it. I couldn't believe that I was letting all of those comments pass by and worse, I would laugh them off even though I knew they were somewhat hurtful. I fully participated in this. I was letting my dad throw jokey, borderline disrespectful comments my way. No wonder I always felt a bit shit about myself after. It took someone from the outside to make me realise it. And yet, at that point, I was still hoping to get my dad's complete approval and validation over what I was doing. The questions: 'How much are you earning? That's just a daytime show, isn't it? Is it a big part? Who's famous in this film you're in, then?' Funnily enough, they didn't make me feel good and yet I kept coming back for more in the hope I could impress him with the next thing I did.

Eventually, I realised that this validation-seeking not only didn't lead to anywhere fulfilling, but I did not actually need it in order to pursue my career and be happy with what I'd achieved. It was also a wake-up call; I had to talk to Dad.

The next day, he called me saying how lovely it was to meet my boyfriend and that he hoped he had made a good impression on him. That was when I decided to not avoid what was on my mind anymore. I managed to have an honest chat about the way he was making me feel. He was very shocked because he hadn't realised how he was speaking to me. He fully apologised and made sure I knew how proud he was of what I had accomplished and done with my life so far. There is such a thing as an honest, humble, grounded conversation between child and parent. I was really happy I had finally told him how I was feeling and that he had acknowledged his errors. Since then, our catch-ups come from a place of honesty and humanity. It's quite heart-warming to see how far we have come.

The day you realise that your parent isn't perfect, makes mistakes and is human is quite surprising, in a good way. You no longer put them on a pedestal and there is a real opportunity to bond with them in a new, grown-up, more mature way. Of course, sometimes the mistakes made are too difficult to overcome and the healthier option is to remove yourself from that situation completely. And more power to you for choosing yourself and your happiness. But there is still a lesson there. Always. Whether you have much admiration for how they live and want to replicate that in your life or decide that that is not how you want to live your life. On both sides, you've got nothing to lose by observing them.

If I'm being honest, I have learnt more from the broken, angry, flawed moments in my family than through the good ones. Don't get me wrong, I am completely 100 percent lucky. I have a family that I can share my life with and be myself with and I do not take that for granted in any way. I've got myself some serious allies, a bond and a support system for a lifetime. But let's face it, when the relationship needs work, when it's challenging, when there is conflict, friction, misunderstandings, jealousy, resentment and judgement, that's where real resilience, endurance, independence and strength in yourself are built. It just is. It might feel tough in the moment of conflict, but it will help you grow into the person you are meant to be. That's when the real hardcore building of character kicks in.

I do believe that our families are meant to teach us and help us grow into the person we're meant to be. My parents taught me a hell of a lot, but not in the way I expected. It didn't occur to me, until I was about 22, that my parents could *actually* be wrong about some things. I just assumed parents were designed to know everything about life and decision-making. Quite the mistake. Everyone has their unique experience with their parents of course, but one of the biggest realisations of my twenties was to find out that my parents don't always have it together. And that's OK. They will mess up, make mistakes, and be vulnerable but in very different and fascinating ways. I've personally never met two more polar opposite people than my folks; it's quite absurd actually. Baffling how they even got together in the first place.

I think their divorce lawyer would agree on that one.

So, when I turned 30, this is what I did. I sat down and made a list of what they'd taught me so far. I like to think that, by then, I knew them well enough and had observed enough to take a step back and get some perspective on the lessons I learnt. Obviously, this is an always-evolving relationship, but I embraced the 30-milestone and ran with it.

I would love it if you could do the same, no matter where your relationship lies with them now, no matter what age you're at; it certainly is an eye-opening exercise. It'll make you reflect on the lessons that came out of the disagreements, the fights, the misunderstandings, and the frustrations but also out of the tender supportive moments, the emotional revelations and the unconditional love.

Briefly, this is what I have got from them so far.

Dad, the ambitious, charismatic, stubborn, funny Englishman from Oxford, has taught me about imperfection, strength, risk-taking, forgiveness, resilience, pain and the power of faith. He grounds me. I cherish our monthly lunch dates in Cecconi's more than he knows. I'll keep observing and learning from him, the good and the bad. I'll take it all. I also learned that, even though my expectations weren't always met, he does his very best and that's all I can ask for. I don't always like him, but I do love him. And I think he would say the same about me. I pin that down to us being way more similar and having much more in common than we'd like to admit. It hasn't always been pleasant but that's when the lessons and growth are most noticeable for me. I am very grateful for him.

Mum, the beautiful, sensitive, stubborn French woman from Paris, has taught me about complete and unconditional love, honesty, beauty, boldness, elegance, kindness, being true to my absolute self and pure laughter. *You know that kind of laughter that hurts your stomach and makes you ugly cry with joy, UGH, just the best.* She's my steady hand; no one knows me quite like she does and that will always be the case. She's the biggest blessing and a huge, bright light in everyone's lives. She frustrated me for most of my twenties because I thought she deserved better than what she settled for. She is not a risk-taker, either, and I struggle with that. She is content with very little and my wanting more for her is just something I have to sit with. I wish my kicking her in the butt would work sometimes. Her stubbornness is unparalleled. My learning to let go and accept her decisions is still a work in progress. She puts off doing every single thing that could be an inconvenience. I've also learnt not to believe her when she says she'll 'get round to it.' She won't.

It's quite tricky to put into words how much my mother means to me and how much of a pillar in my life she is. We are joined in a very strong, intense, potentially over-the-top manner and we always have been. Even during my teenage years, she was my best friend and I didn't realise how out of the ordinary that was. It's a pretty unique bond. We will often call each other at the exact same second. We talk every day even if it's about nothing. I will yell at her while also hugging her and vice versa. She frustrates me and inspires me. She's one to tell me I'm perfect just the way I am when I'm struggling with my body. She'll also tell me when I look like crap and need to get my shit together. She can party until 3 am with my friends and create game quizzes about awkward sexual experiences. *I don't think my friends fully recovered from that evening.* There is very little we don't share with each other.

I told her about that time I broke my vagina at the gym, *long story*, and I thought I had to go to A&E, and she told me when she had an affair with someone she shouldn't have. She can't cook but tries. Everyone has a crush on her but she has no idea. She can paint beautifully, and write beautifully, but doesn't think she can. However, when it comes to me, and my brother, we can do anything in her eyes. When I say she's a huge light, I am not lying. Some friends that have only met her once, will always ask about her and how she's doing. I could go on and on, but I think you get the gist.

If you have a family member like that, please make sure you let them know how important they are to you. You only get one, if you're lucky.

So yeah! My parents have given me so many life lessons so far. Neither of them taught me how to cook, unfortunately. *Beans on toast anyone?* No matter how small of an influence parents might've had on you until now, take their influences and make them your own. Of course, this isn't limited to parents. Maybe another family member will have more impact, will raise you, and will be more of a parent than a mother and father could be.

Speaking of which, grandparents are an absolute gift, aren't they? Oh, how I wish everyone could meet my French grandmother, Mamie Renée. She's my hero, the shining star of the family. She's 82 and has more energy, beauty, strength and radiance shining out of her now than I've ever seen. After my grandfather died, ending a very troublesome and sad marriage, I think my grandmother took the opportunity to truly live the way my grandfather had never allowed her to. It seemed that with his death, she was reborn. She now goes ballroom dancing, matches her outfits to her jewellery, goes to the hair salon every week AND has had three relationships in eight years. *Her love life is more entertaining, scandalous and thrilling than mine will ever be*. Currently, she is with a lovely man ten years younger than her. *Can we say GOALS?*

She is a true light. I will always aspire to be like she is: pure goodness and sparkle. Every time I speak with her, I learn something new. She makes me laugh like no other and astonishes me with her natural beauty and spontaneous way of simply *being*. And yes, she will also spend the entire phone call asking us to repeat ourselves because she refuses to get a hearing aid. 'It's for old people and I am NOT old,' she says. But that's OK. I love listening to her stories; she always has the most outrageous ones.

If you are lucky to still have a grandparent, do savour the little moments with them, it's the most precious time you'll get. They've lived through more than you could imagine and will teach you a tremendous amount. Grandparents have this ability to make you appreciate the present when you're with them because you don't know how much time you'll have left with them. *Wouldn't it be nice if we could apply that all the time?*

How about next time you are sitting with a grandparent, stop for a second and try to bottle that feeling of being completely present and grateful for that moment and then implement that feeling as much as you can in your daily life. Ultimately, the present is all we have, and our grandparents are a reminder of that. It's a real gift.

Siblings are also a joy and a piece of work at the same time. I didn't really get along with my little – *now so tall* – brother. We were born four years apart. We had different interests and when it comes to our personalities, we are polar opposites. As we grew into our teenage years, we didn't always get along. There was a solid understanding that we just had different interests and that would be that. And yet, I have always felt very protective of him; I have always been supportive and have always been there if he needed it. There is a bond. *I think the fact that I was in charge of his 18th birthday party and the cops showed up because of the noise, while my mum was away, bonded us even more, if I'm honest.*

However, through my twenties and as he entered his twenties, we've learned to lean on each other in some important moments. We do have a deep appreciation and great admiration for one another. Our relationship has definitely grown into something special. We also realise that even though we might not have much in common, what we do have is a shared childhood and memories – that doesn't mean we still don't clash at times, though.

My brother has his faults, like everyone else. I don't always understand his process in life but I respect it and watch him, in, *silent*, admiration. He just fascinates me. Not only is he an already well-established pastry chef, who does modelling on the side, *with a jawline that could cut glass*, but he's also the kind of guy who, by the age of 26, had a secure job that he enjoyed, a sports car, had bought a house and has consistently had stable relationships since he was 16. He also has a dog, two cats and a snake. *Don't ask.* You can imagine who the favourite child is between the two of us. *I do not have the time or energy to tell that part of the story and besides, I'm much wiser now; I let go of things. I'm not jealous. I'm not.*

Next to him, I am absolute chaos. My life is the opposite of stable; it's messy and unpredictable. My brother likes an ordered way of living but does have an edge to him too. *Did I mention the snake?* And has many contradictions to him, too. As much as he enjoys stability, he also completely lives on the edge when it comes to money. We don't operate the same way in that regard. My brother is a risk-taker when it comes to money. Big time. But with that, he also has this freakishly calm faith that things will just work out. He rarely gets stressed out because he follows his instincts without much doubt in his mind. I really wish I could be more like that. *Don't tell him that, though.*

In watching him grow up, he's taught me that there's a lot more strength in the calm and grounded way of living. Unlike me, he doesn't have that chaotic energy in his brain. He focuses his energy, makes a decision and goes for it. I aspire to use some of that instead of the constant back and forth of 'Oh but what if it doesn't work, what if I hate it, what if I'm not good enough, what if it's not for me, what if I fail, what if I don't have enough money.' *Sound familiar to anyone? Just me? OK, great.*

I do think everyone could benefit a little from his philosophy, take a page from his book. Don't think of reasons why you can't do it, just do it. Calm your mind, focus and things clear up. *And suddenly you're surrounded by cats, dogs, a snake in a new house and a new car. Easy peasy guys, come on.* As different as we are, we have something I didn't anticipate growing up: a very deep mutual respect for one another. Even though we lead very different lives, we cheer each other on and if you can find that support in your siblings and put aside the differences, you may realise that it's a pretty special bond to have. If you are open to it.

And hey, it's OK not to get along with family relatives; there is no need to keep toxic people in your life if you can help it. But if there is a way to build something there, why not? Ask yourself why you ended up in your particular family? What did you benefit from them and keep benefitting from now? Is there something you're supposed to be learning from them? Think about it.

Overall, if there is one huge thing my family has taught me, it's forgiveness... and unconditional support. Every single person in my family, at some point, has made a mistake. I've observed so many different family dynamics, on both sides of the pond. Someone's either hurt someone, they've not listened, lied, cheated, had fights, been drunk, not spoken for years, and yet, every single person, no matter how long it took, has forgiven the other person. And that's big. That's something I didn't really think was possible to overcome at times. Some issues seem unforgivable. But I've seen my family patiently and beautifully come back together and cherish each other in a human, honest way.

Now, your turn. What has your family taught you?

One of the best parts of my twenties was not only having a grander perspective on my family members – *and leaving the family house... no offence Mum, but I had to go* – but also being able to choose and build a family of my own. *No, no I don't mean babies.* The people we carefully hand-pick and give our trust to; Friends.

Friends: The Family You Choose (Wisely)

Let's get straight to the point. My friends are what got me through my twenties. No two ways about it. They have shaped me into the person I am today and if there is one thing I can be proud of, it is the fact that I chose pretty inspiring, one-of-a-kind, wonderful people as my friends. *I'm so grateful they haven't stopped taking my calls yet.*

The people you choose to have in your life will define a lot of what makes your life what it is. You can't go through all of this on your own. You can try, but I don't believe it'll lead to a happy and fulfilling life. You need to share your life with people who let you be you and are going to be on your side, cheering you on. And vice versa.

Writing this chapter has really made me ask myself quite a lot of questions about friendships and all the people we meet along the way. Why do some people stick? How do they shape who we are and how do they impact us? I have no idea how all of us come to find our friends, our best mates, our confidantes, we just do. You bump into them somehow and it just sticks. They are there to stay. Maybe it's fate.

I knew from an early age that my friendships were going to be one of the most important things I could have in my life. Even as a teenager, I always prioritised building and sustaining friendships over romantic relationships. It's true what they say: guys/girls can come and go, but a true friendship lasts a lifetime and will be with you through thick and thin. This means I have friendships that go back 15 years and I cherish that. I had a strong feeling that building trustworthy, dependable, special friendships was going to be a huge contribution to my fulfilment and happiness. And I was right. My life would be far less fun and entertaining without my friends in it.

However, finding true friends is no easy task. It can take years. It certainly did for me. I moved to London not knowing a single soul. And I had to go through a lot of 'friendships' to find my peeps. Figuring out who to trust, who to be completely yourself with, and who to share your life experiences with, is tough. And you might not always get it right. Some people just don't have your best interest at heart. There are a lot of jealous, mean-spirited, insecure people out there, people who can take advantage of you. The ones that appear to be friends at the beginning and who turn out to be disappointments. In order to avoid these kinds of these let downs, here are a few things I picked up along the way that helped me figure out the meaning of true friendship:

How someone reacts when you succeed or when you have good news to share will be *very* telling of how much of a friend they are. Observe what they do and what they say. It's simple: if they are truly happy for you, if they help you celebrate your wins, those ones are the keepers. Those are the ones you can trust and listen to.

Beware of a 'friend' who loves to be the first one there to comfort you when you're down but can't stand to celebrate with you when you win. They are not your friend. Real friends will listen to the bad news and carry you through it but won't derail the conversation to make it about them or enjoy the comforting part a little too much. They are meant to be your cheerleaders and your comfort peeps all in one. Real friends want what is best for you and want you to be happy. And vice versa.

Pay attention to how much effort is put into the friendship on both sides. If you feel like you are always the one who is messaging, organising meet-ups and generally putting more effort into seeing the person, the balance is lost and it might be time to reassess if this person is really interested in being your friend. Or is it only when it suits them? You deserve to have a friend who puts as much time into the friendship as you do. Your time is precious, spend it with people who see that.

As you grow older, you enter a Less Bullshit Zone. People you *choose* to have in your life are meant to inspire you, mentor you, motivate you and support you. Generally, friends are meant to bring positive energy into your life. If what they bring is negativity, jealousy, narcissism or laziness, I would suggest letting go of those people. You'll realise that it might be time to cut them out and move on. If someone makes you feel less of yourself, if you feel you need to shine less for them to take that sparkle, if you feel they are not willing to celebrate good news and relish the moments in the bad news. OUT, they must go. Try not to give in to that energy. That is not friendship. It seems obvious, and yet, we all have a few people in our lives where it has taken a little too long to realise their true colours. *Don't worry, you will figure that out.*

There comes a time when our standards become higher: we simply pay more attention to how people make us feel and if that serves us in a good way in our lives. And here's the thing. You don't need a ton of friends. You just need a few great ones. People who inspire you, who aspire for you to be better, who make you feel supported and loved. People you can learn from. And who are a laugh to be around! *If you're not laughing about something stupid, what are you doing?* Those folks are worth your time.

That said, there will be something I like to call 'friendship levels'. They are usually pretty clear and recognising those levels will then help measure your expectations.

We have the friends who are just there to have fun. The Going Out friends, the on-the-surface-level mates. You go out with them, party with them, have light, stupid conversations with them. But they are not the ones you're going to call up when you need a serious conversation, some guidance or some real support. These are the ones you call up when you feel like having some light fun socialising, gossip about who slept with who and what's the next place we're going to go out. You usually won't know a lot, if anything, really important about them. And this suits everyone just fine. It's nice to have those people, it's an escape and comes with very little expectations from them. Easy breezy. *Those friendships usually end when you realise you have nothing in common or have outgrown their lifestyle.*

Then, we've got the Old Friends. The ones you see maybe once a year but it'll always remain a special bond because you have your teenage experiences in common. You follow each other from a distance and always have the same rapport when you meet again. You attend their weddings, you see them when you're in the same town, you reminisce about university drunken days and it's special. They know who you were and can remind you of that. It's comforting to know we will always be in each other's lives without having to see them in person all the time. It's easy and heartwarming. Don't forget those people you grew up with. Nostalgia brings people together. Even if it's just once a year.

If you happen to have a romantic life partner, then I hope you can call them your friend as well. Actually, if I'm honest, they would probably, *hopefully*, have to be up there on the best friend list. If you're not having the best laughs, the best chats, and a desire to share the whole experience of your lives with each other, then what are you doing?! There has to be friendship at the core of it, too. Those are my expectations at least. Let's face it: liking the person you're with is just as important as loving them.

I know it's maybe cheating because she's also family but my mum is one of my favourite people on this planet. *If the description earlier wasn't clear enough.* She is my most precious confidant and her friendship has been the biggest blessing in my life. Hear that, ladies? Mums can be best friends too! They more than qualify for the job – the wisest women out there in my opinion!

Then, you have your Platonic Guy Friends. The dudes. The testosterone viewpoint. A key element in a girl's life. Growing up, in high school, I had quite a few guy friends. I enjoyed hanging out with them, playing cards and ping-pong in between classes. I think I just liked the simplicity of how guys function. Fairly straightforward, no overthinking. If there's a ball or a video game, they are happy. Obviously, there would occasionally be the 'awkward' conversation, when feelings started getting in the way, but most of the time we just moved on and enjoyed being teenagers without any fuss. Things got a bit trickier with those guys after high school when their jealous girlfriends or wives would not understand or accept the whole 'she's just a friend from high school' spiel. *I don't see those guys anymore. Shame.*

In my twenties, though, I got really lucky with the dudes who became friends. *That's right, good men do exist, ladies!* I am happy to say I have a couple of solid good guy friends and they do enrich my life. They give me the guys' perspective, which is SO different from how we women, think. There is a lot less faffing about, it's a very straightforward approach to life. *Aggravatingly straightforward at times, let's be honest.* They've also taught me a hell of a lot when it comes to guys and what everything means in their world. And I like to think I've taught them about what the hell goes on in our minds too. *Don't worry I've always defended our truth, girls.* If you can, I would really recommend finding at least one guy, platonically. One you can reach out to when you need some testosterone advice. They might surprise you.

One of my dude friends certainly did. I have known him for seven-plus years and he often describes me as heart-warming, very mature and yet very guarded. He is very good at reminding me how I've grown and what I've accomplished. And that's what has surprised me. Guys observe more than we think. He picks up on things and puts me back in my place when I need to, in a way some of my gal pals can't. I remember this particular moment when he smashed out the best quotes ever during quite a sad time in my life.

A time when I was quite heartbroken and hadn't told anyone yet. We were out in a bar that week with a few friends. He saw that I was sad and down. I don't remember this at all, but he remembers me saying that I didn't want to be weak and show I was sad at that time. It seemed I was carrying a lot of weight on my shoulders, not wanting to burden, even my friends, and certainly not admitting I was a bit beaten down. He remembered being surprised by my guardedness and when I told him I was done with men for a long while, he decided to share the time he was heartbroken. Someone had asked him 'Do you think you'll ever love again? Could you ever love again?' He then, very simply, replied: 'Well, what's the alternative? Not feeling anything? I'd rather feel everything, every emotion, every feeling, even hurt, instead of feeling nothing.' It was a beautiful moment. He managed to lift my spirits and make me feel like it was going to be ok.

Guy Friends: I love you, mates! You're still gross but you're alright.

Finally, we've got the level of friendship that really took me by surprise in its profoundness and necessity, the mother of all friendships, the one that's deserving of its own heading in this chapter: Hardcore Female Friends.

The Beauty Of Female Friendships

I like to call them my soul sisters. The ones you meet and you know they're going to be it. The 'No bullshit' level. It's hilarious, beautiful and important.

I cannot speak enough about the importance of female friendships in a gal's life. Female friendships are pretty much the best relationships you'll ever have and you do need to make sure you nurture them, especially from your twenties onwards.

When I moved to London, I could only have dreamed about finding a group of girls I would go through my twenties with, a bunch of girls that would enrich my life and guide me in every way possible. Women who were smart, complex, like-minded, outspoken, loud, messy, and beautiful inside and out. Girls who knew me sometimes better than I knew myself... WELL, I hit the bloody jackpot in that department.

Let me give you a little glimpse into our friendship.

A few days ago, a high-school mate of mine, who lives in my hometown in France and works in a shoe shop, sent me a video of him going through every room of his brand new four-bedroom house that he just bought with his boyfriend. It was a Tuesday night, I was eating way too many M&Ms and deciding if I should even bother with dinner. I was not ready to see this video. One of my oldest friends became a full-on, settled, house-owner adult, while I was drowning in chocolate. Nope. He sends me this and I have some sort of overly dramatic pitiful reaction. I crack open the red wine and, as usual, send a pitiful voice note to two of my gals, which went something along the lines of:

I just wanted to say that I thought I was having a really good Monday and then So-and-So messages me with a video of this fucking huge house that he's just bought with his boyfriend and he's done a full tour of the house and I'm having some sort of identity crisis where I'm nowhere near buying a fucking huge house. How has this happened? I'm happy with my really good room in London and he's just bought a four-bedroom house with this huge garden and everything is brand new. So, yeah, that's all I have to say, I'm really upset. Should I just go back to my hometown and shack up with someone there? Is it time?

These are the two responses I got from my ever-supportive, Slap-In-The-Face, Shut-Up-Already friends. Two very different and yet hilarious responses. Word for word, not making this up.

Sara, ever-loving, guru-like, supportive, would jump in the river to save me, friend:

Well, would that make you happy? What is it you really dream of? Being an actress, enjoying life, or being in your small hometown with a massive house, just you and someone else? I don't know. Everybody is at different stages in life. Some people have quiet lives with houses, babies and routines. Everybody misses out on something. Yes, they have houses, but they couldn't write a book. You have a lot of stories to tell and that's thanks to all the experiences you've been exposed to because of the choices that you've made. So you're here now, you are happy with what you've got. Be happy for him. You'll get there one day. You'll find somebody. You'll be able to have a plan together and buy a house, or let him buy it, so you can keep your money. The good thing is that you have all those options open to you; you're free, and you haven't committed to anything. He's not, he has a massive mortgage probably and he's committed to this other man. You never know. Just look at what makes you happy, look at your story and how amazing it is.

Louise, ever sarcastic, enough-is-enough, no-bullshit friend, would not jump in the river for me but would attempt to find a hot dude to come and save me:

OK, so Number One. You do know it's Tuesday right? Just putting that one out there. Number Two, unless So-and-So has been saving every penny he's been earning from the shoe shop, has he now got a massive mortgage? Has he just indebted himself? It might not be all that fucking rosy. And what's he doing with a four-bed house anyway? Is it one for all his fucking cats? What? Uh? Um? And hey, homeownership sucks. Coming from someone who knows. Too much to maintain. You're not ready for all of that. Don't go back to Brittany. Take his house as a place you can crash on a holiday. A room in London is not that bad. Low maintenance, comfortable, nice part of town, you're not doing so badly. But if you want to go and do what he does, then do it for a while... Then, your mum and I will come to visit you at the asylum you'll evidently end up in. And I'm sure that would be nice. We'd get you a room with a view or something. I'll keep thinking. I'm sure I'll come up with other reasons why this is a BAD IDEA.

And there you have it. A couple of my gals. I needed those two responses. This is a small example of course but if you can find people who will tell you exactly what you need to hear, you're on the right track in your friendships.

It's the oversharing, overly supportive, flawed, funny kind. It's calling you out when you're being a bitch, making you laugh when you need it, calling you when they sense your texts are off. You can be gloriously yourself and that's all you can ever hope for.

I am very lucky and grateful. My friends let me be my true, authentic self, all the bloody time. They let me cry, laugh, complain, get angry, be selfish, be ugly, be beautiful, be a terrible singer in public, be free, be me, all the time. They support me through thick and thin, *even when I'm driving a car... it's* baffling. They give the best hugs, make the best roast dinners, the best drinks – *apart from you Sara, your tea is despicable, darling* – make me smile even when I'm sad, calm me down on the phone when I'm having a panic attack, send me podcasts I'll like, send me books when I'm in a slump, bring me cake, tuck me in bed when I'm too drunk, protect me at all costs; force me, when I'm hungover, to queue for The Breakfast Club brunch because 'It'll be worth the pain of queuing' and ends up being the best brunch I've ever had, *I still cannot be in a queue without complaining, though, and I think I never will, it's my French side OK?*, send me ridiculous videos that'll make me piss myself, sneak me into a concert without tickets, make a bangin' playlist on Spotify during Covid Times, chat about anything and everything, including hilarious sex conversations that involve best condoms, red flags, size, root for each other when one of us has had great sex – *I'm talking the embarrassing jumping up and down congratulatory dance kind of support...* I could go ON and ON. I wish these kinds of friendships on everyone. They are pretty special.

My friends are pure gold. They come from all walks of life and make my life full in so many beautiful ways. Choosing friends who are different from you is something that will keep you grounded. Because how great is it to see the world through different lenses, and have different points of view and guidance from the people you trust the most? It's what makes friendship so rich and interesting.

Friendship is a two-way street. Your friends are going to be your pillars throughout your life. Make damn sure you take care of them, carefully and lovingly.

And if there is one nice thing I can say about myself is that I make sure I can also be the best friend I can be.

The beautiful thing about friendship is that YOU choose each other. You could've picked anyone in the world, but you picked each other; you chose to be in each other's lives and share experiences and life moments, laughs, cries and everything in between. YOU decided to let them in your little world and the trust you share with them is one of a kind. You can be gloriously yourself and that's all you can ever hope for. You can watch *Sex and the City*, or *Friends*, and only dream of similar friendships. But when they actually happen to you, when you happen to be in a room, laughing, screaming, cheering each other on, sharing outrageous sex stories, crying in each other's arms over anxiety, stress, boys, life, work, you can feel nothing but gratitude for that.

Cherishing moments with your friends is also vital, simply because you don't get those moments back. And boy, sometimes I wish I could revisit some of the hilarity we went through in our twenties. That time we went clubbing and strangers got so drunk that they paid us to stand next to a stool full of coats because they thought I was the cloakroom gal. Stealing balloons from a bar and travelling with them on the Tube because we were upset it was not our birthday. House parties that ended two days later with unexplainable bruises and questionable photos. Dancing on a table in a club and ripping the projector sheet while falling flat on our faces. Going to the Cannes Film Festival and pretending my friend was my manager in order to get into events. Dancing in Kensington Gardens and getting everyone around us to join in. Witnessing my friend kick a guy out of my flat because he was shady and wanted to be alone with me in a room is up there in most-badass-things-I-have-seen. Most recently, having my girls in one room for my 30th, during the pandemic, going round the table, each of us saying what we've learned so far and what we are grateful for. Precious moments that become amazing memories. When I turned 30, I vowed to stop and appreciate the moments when they are there; they are pretty special. The sharing, the comforting, the reassuring, the banter, the bonding, the endless talks. You can't bottle that – you have to create it.

What surprises me is that I didn't think I'd find people who know me better than I know myself and yet I've learned that my girls do actually pay attention and believe in me in ways I sometimes don't. *And if you don't do this already, please listen to your gals more when they guide you, because 9 times out of 10, they KNOW what is best for you.*

I know how lucky I am because it wasn't a quick, smooth-sailing ride. It took me years to find these kinds of friends. They didn't come easily and they took a while to fully flourish into amazing friendships. None of them came into my life by accident but they did come from very unpredictable places. I mention this because I think it's important to be open to friendships, anywhere, anytime because you CAN find a truly special friend in the most random of places. I certainly did!

You'd think, being an actor, that I probably met my friends on a film set or in castings. It would be such a nice, predictable story. Nope. I met my friends working with them on jobs I did BETWEEN acting. Meaning, working at a bar trying to sell Jaegermeister keychains, *yes you read that correctly, keychains,* working at medical conferences giving the microphone to surgeons in a conference room trying not to fall asleep during their speeches, being an elf at the Christmas Grotto and her being the manager knowing that this job was going to ruin me if it was taken seriously, promoting at a vape show, even though neither of us had ever smoked, working on a random music video where neither of us knew the singer. Those kinds of jobs. I don't regret any of those gigs because they brought me the friends I have today. Even though at the time, I wondered what the hell I was doing with my life, I now know exactly how the universe was working. It's utterly ridiculous. If my acting career had been thriving at any of these points in my life, I would not have met these girls. And that is quite inconceivable.

Wherever you are in your life, be open to friendships. Be open to finding them anywhere, anytime because you never know. In the middle of a shitty job, a doctor's waiting room, a supermarket, a gym class, there can be your person. There is no time limit on finding your best friend, you just have to be open to it and realise how beautiful and important having a friend is.

I'll say it again: Female friendships are the most important relationships you'll have. They are unbreakable bonds. There is a beautiful quote in *Sex and the City*: "Why don't we be each other's soulmates? And men can just be people we have a good time with?" That's a pretty sweet plan if you ask me.

"Girlfriends are like trees: strong, grounded, capable of handling great storms, wise and most of all they are oxygen." – ***Amber Valletta.***

AUNTY ANGE TIPS

- Call your grandparents more often.

- Make a list of what your family has taught you. Especially through the bad stuff.

- Let go of unnecessary drama in the family. The little things don't matter. *See Mum and Dad, I didn't even mention that my brother is clearly the favourite. No drama.*

- Support your friends in every way possible. That also means letting them make their own mistakes. Painful but necessary.

- You don't need 25 friends who barely know you. One is enough, one who can tell you to shut up when you're being annoying and tell you they love you when you need it.

- I don't know who needs to hear this but if a friend of yours makes you feel less of yourself, shitty or insecure, newsflash: they are not your friend. Thank you, next.

- Friendship is a two-way street. If you're alone doing the work, call them out or move on.

- Cherish and work on your friendships. They are the gems that hold everything together.

- Be open to finding friendships, wherever and whenever you are in life.

VI. TAMING ANXIETY

W e all deal with a certain level of stress or anxiety at some stage in our lives. I have not yet encountered a human being who is immune to it and I am certainly no exception. I have freakin' mastered the art of anxiety – worrying about imaginary scenarios that will never happen, discovering the *wonderful* symptoms of panic attacks, swearing off anyone who brought up meditation and breathing...until I actually listened.

Your twenties are a particular source of stress and overwhelming emotion. There have been moments where I have felt so lost and confused about what I was supposed to accomplish that most of the time I felt like I was failing. It's a pretty common feeling. Unrealistic expectations. We are hard on ourselves because we think we're supposed to know what the hell we're doing and have all the answers, which means ups and downs are inevitable, as is stress.

Anxiety is something I didn't know anything about until it happened to land on me. It took me by surprise, but it was certainly not unprovoked. Turns out, if you don't deal with your emotions, feelings, childhood and general issues with the past, they tend to pop up, unexpectedly and ferociously, causing anxiety. It's not pleasant, desired or well-received, but it is needed in order to steer things back towards a way of life that is more enjoyable and peaceful. Aside from all the hellish crap anxiety put me through, it did force me to sit down and assess what the hell was going on. And I like to think that my attitude, thought process and general outlook on life are much better for it.

To rise above it all, I had to go through it. I had to understand and pinpoint where the anxiety was coming from and find the tools to deal with it. Like everything else, it is still a work in progress. But there is hope! Here's what I've found out so far that might also be able to help you guys out.

Damn You, Stress!

I think we can all agree: stress is an absolute bitch. There's no other way to describe it really. It's just this tedious, ongoing, relentless, harrowing thing – something we are never really told about until it pops up and does some damage.

What's really great is that it can manifest itself at any given point in your life. *Hopefully, you'll have caught on to the very sarcastic tone of this book... otherwise I apologise.*

Stress can start young. I've noticed that children are prone to absorb everything that surrounds them. They soak up a lot of the energy that exists around them. If they grow up in a stressful, unstable, chaotic environment, they can become very stressed-out kids themselves. That said, some kids grow up in a perfectly calm, peaceful setting and will be just as stressed later in life, if not more so. I'm no psychologist, but there seems to be no logic or reason.

Teenagers might have it the worst when it comes to stress and anxiety, though. Boy, do I NOT miss being one myself. On top of going through the hormonal changes, puberty and the joyful zits that come with it, as well as experiencing many firsts, they have to deal with exams, homework, the pressure parents put on them – or the pressure they put on themselves – whilst also figuring out a suitable career path that will make them happy, fulfilled and earn them money. Makes me feel stressed just remembering the sheer mess of it all. No thanks.

But then, right when you're done with exams and university life, and you think you've managed to just about get away with some major life moments, adulthood hits you in the face and stress comes up with a whole new bunch of ways to manifest itself again. It takes many exciting forms. There are various degrees of stress of course, but most symptoms include irritability, anger, fatigue, muscle pain, digestive troubles, and difficulty sleeping. I'm sure you recognise a few of these. It ain't no picnic.

And yes, you're right, this is a rant. Stress is not my friend.

I think I've always been quite a stressed-out person, even when I thought I wasn't, but the first time I encountered real stress was in school.

In high school, I used to be so hard on myself. Even when I studied well for a test, I would panic the day before. It really does feel like life or death when you're in it, though, at least, it did for me. Obviously, once you're out of it, you realise school was nothing compared to what life was going to throw at you. Still, school can really put your nerves through the wringer. For my Baccalaureate finals, I remember being so sick to my stomach the night before, so unable to shake off my nerves, that my mum told me to go outside, walk to the cornfield next door to our house, and run around as fast as I could. She said, 'it's a great way to let off steam.' I'm pretty sure she secretly wanted me out of the house, sick of seeing my painful state. But I went along with it. I ran around this cornfield like a crazy person. And it helped, for a minute. Until I puked in the field and walked back feeling even worse.

Sometimes, the stress of failing a test would be so strong that I would fake an illness or pretend to feel faint to get out of it. Mum, if you're reading this now, I'm sorry. I just couldn't handle the pain it caused me. That block in the stomach, the headaches and lack of sleep. Ugh, it's exhausting, and no one really tells you how to manage it all when you're growing up. You just sit with it and hope that it will slowly calm down.

What's funny now is that I distinctly remember one of my teachers telling me, a few weeks before my final exams, that I should save some of that stress for 'real life' – aka 'after school ends and the adult stuff kicks in.' I truly thought that he was wrong. Surely, this kind of stress wouldn't occur after school. After school meant freedom. It meant happiness! Haha, oh how innocent I was...or stupid. Big surprise, stress definitely doesn't end there. Nope.

I graduated with honours, from high school and after a couple of fun years at university, I decided to pursue my dream career of acting, in London. It was a bold move, but I knew it would make me happy. Except this meant that I was moving to a foreign city, without knowing a single soul, and with not a single job lined up. Kind of delusional if you ask me now but hey, I was 19, driven and passionate.

So now, little me has to deal with way more important things than school grades. I have to actually earn money, manage that money, pay bills, pay taxes, cook for myself, find work, progress in my work, manage time for my family and friends, go on dates, avoid getting pregnant or catching STDs, book my own doctor appointments, etc. Stress truly shines in these moments, doesn't it? It's glorious. I finally understood what that bloody teacher meant. I wish he had expanded a bit more on stress in adulthood. Can't say he didn't warn me, though. Cheeky bugger.

It's not something we sign up for and yet this stuff is what we ALL deal with on a daily basis. Juggling it all seems impossible at times and quite overwhelming. Stress covers a whole bunch of crap, but I would say all of us have specific things that really get to us, too. Personally, two things strongly affect my stress levels: money and castings.

Ugh, money. It really is a source of stress for so many of us, isn't it? I don't have a miracle cure for financial anxiety, I'm sorry to say. I have quite an unusual relationship with money. I think it might have to do with how I was raised, and a few things that were ingrained in me as a teenager, that have spilled into my adult life.

When I was a child, my family was quite well-off. My parents had great jobs and money was never a concern. Then, my parents got divorced and my dad left his well-paid job to build his own business. I saw my mum struggle, month to month, working in a primary school. Money did not flow like it used to. And even though my brother and I never missed out on anything as kids and teenagers, my mother's concerns over money must have lingered long enough for me to pick up on it and apply this frugal mindset in my adult life. I also have two very upper-class grandparents who reminded me, every chance they got, to save money and never spend a penny on anything useless. Every grocery shopping experience with them involved holding their 25 vouchers in one hand and picking up ONLY the two-for-one items in the supermarket. Ingrained, I'm telling you. I guess that's how they stayed rich.

For these reasons, money has always subconsciously been associated with worry, for me. In my early twenties, I used to get very stressed about it, pretty much on a weekly basis, although to be fair, it was justified by the fact that I had little acting work coming my way at the time and sky-high London rent to pay. I think we can all agree those were good excuses for concern. But at other times, and I still catch myself doing it today, I worry about money just out of habit. I worry even when I have money in my bank account, which is insane, I know. I am well aware of my insane irrational brain. In my defence, In my defence, I have an unstable life. It's an unstable life. I never know when my next job is going to be. My next paycheck could be months away. So, in that sense, I justify the worry, even when I really shouldn't. My friends have learnt over time to just go with these irrational concerns of mine, although they do occasionally hint at the concept of me and therapy sessions...Might take them up on that idea... soonish.

And before you say 'Oh boy this girl is nuts, why would she possibly worry about money that's actually in her bank account.' Well, let me tell you. A lot of the things we stress about are NOT rational. You can have a root canal that needs fixing but you're scared shitless of the dentist. You're gonna stress about the appointment for days even though you know that the dentist probably knows what he's doing and you will most probably survive it. Irrational yes, but it doesn't make it any less real. One of my friends absolutely stresses out about calling the doctor to make an appointment. She has to write down some sort of dialogue on paper before dialling... She never sticks to the paper, but it helps her somehow. I'm sure you guys can come up with many more examples of irrational, stress-led behaviour. It doesn't have to make sense for the symptoms to be there. We are irrational beings. Which is my answer to most things when I'm doing something that makes zero sense to others.

Castings. This is, admittedly, quite a niche concern that not many will be dealing with. *You are all sane, well-adjusted people who didn't choose acting as a profession. Well done you.* Over time, I have accepted that nerves in castings can be useful and are simply part of the deal. In the beginning, though, I was a blubbering mess. Every casting felt like I was dealing with life and death. The stakes were momentous; the pressure was immeasurable – 'If I don't get this job, I am a piece of shit and the world will collapse' kind of pressure. It was probably evident to everyone in the casting room, and who wants to give a job to a shaky, sweaty, desperate gal who forgets her lines due to pure stress? No one. Two years into auditioning, I went to see an acting coach, who helped me with this problem.

As a side note, the method I learned can be useful to anyone who has to go through a presentation at work, a job interview or even when someone has to speak about something that's important but becomes an absolute wreck when it comes to public speaking, nerves taking over and making a mess of everything. It doesn't have to be like that. You can use nerves to your advantage. You just have to figure out a way to transform that energy into something positive. And remember, nerves are a good thing, they mean you care. Being nervous can be manageable, I promise. And this is coming from someone who once couldn't string two solid sentences together in front of a film director. I remember walking into a very prestigious casting room where this very famous director was attending, shaking from top to bottom. My mind went completely blank when he introduced himself and asked me to sit down. I think my exact words were: 'N...no, yes, OK, I'll sit now. I can sit. Can I sit down? I'm Angélique. Call me Ange. Or what you prefer.' I will spare you the rest of my disastrous mumbling. I could not recognise myself. Safe to say, he couldn't wait to get out of there.

Some sort of intervention was necessary.

Here's what we would do in class. My acting coach would sit me down and force me to breathe deeply in and out for five minutes. He would then tell me to imagine all that nervous energy diving into my two feet, grounding me to the floor. So instead of all that stress up in my head, clouding my brain, it was all rooted in my feet. And this helped me calm my nerves and use that energy from the ground up – not the other way around. If that failed, making a fist in my pocket, releasing and tightening it, was another good trick.

What's important to remember as well is that people are just people. They are human. Everyone gets stressed out about something. Even the big boss. Maybe being upfront and saying that you're a little nervous will help and will show people that you're overcoming something. It makes you human and more endearing to the other person. Obviously, keep those nerves at a healthy level.

It is important to add here that this doesn't mean I'm now miraculously stress-free. That would be like saying I'm currently crapping gold. No, no. Let's make that clear – I'm not even close. But these are useful techniques you can at least try and see if they work for you.

Money and castings aside, I'm also an expert on stressing about things that haven't happened yet. Making up plots in my head of potentially horrible scenarios that haven't happened is my area of expertise.

For example, if my train to the airport is a little late, in my head, that's it. I've missed the plane; the plane is gone. I'm never going to board that plane and watch that Disney movie while eating those shitty peanuts. I'll miss my entire holiday. It's over for me. And then, unsurprisingly, I make it on time and suddenly I'm having Prosecco on the plane completely forgetting what I was worried about only an hour before.

Another one: headaches. Immediately, my brain goes 'You know, you read that article once about that girl that had a headache and then died. Pretty sure that's what you've got.' Or my period is late. 'That's it, I'm having twins and we will all live under a bridge because I can't afford twins.' These are just glimpses of what happens in my brain because if I had to give you a list of all the little things that stress me out daily, the endless worrying about things that haven't happened and probably won't ever, it would be the whole damn book and that's not appealing to anyone, especially me.

How do you think I react when things actually do go wrong? Oh, it's a treat, believe me.

Last year, I had to take the Eurostar from France to London. The journey was already quite a hassle since I was travelling during a pandemic with all the documents and tests required beforehand. But I was going back for work purposes, so I had no choice. On the travel day, my mum was driving me to the station. It was a couple of hours' drive to Paris and we had given ourselves enough time to get there without feeling rushed. Suddenly, the car broke down...on the motorway, an hour into the journey. We were in the middle of nowhere, with no clue how to remain even the slightest bit calm. This had never happened to either of us and let's just say that neither of us handled the situation well. No amount of meditation was going to save us. We were not calm; there was no chill whatsoever. No grace, no feeling grounded. Just pure panic. We were on the side of the road wondering if maybe this wasn't happening, maybe it was a nightmare.

There were tears, curses at the world, certain I was going to miss the acting job in London and that my career would be over. There was nothing cool about it.

Mum, on the other hand, surprised me. After crying hysterically for a few minutes, calling a mechanic and insulting him to kingdom come, she completely switched into Solution Mode. She called her sister who lived 30 minutes away, and who was miraculously free to come and pick us up. I was amazed. *I mean, in the moment, I was numb and shut down, but Mum did impress me after I could feel my body again.* My aunt arrived in her huge Range Rover and my mum drove me to the station, not having a clue how to drive that kind of car, I might add. In the most stressful of situations, she managed to get me to where I needed to be, safely and without breaking a sweat. She smashed it. Never mind that afterwards, she told me she cried for three hours straight, from pure stress, and had most of a bottle of wine to kill her nerves.

In short, you don't want to be either one of us in a crisis. I was an inexplicably uncontrollable, blubbering MESS. I had no perspective about anything. I am so envious of people who are just unfazed in the face of unplanned, stressful situations. They just get on with it, calmly and smoothly. Their heart rates must be golden. Mine definitely hates my guts.

My point here is that, somehow, my mum put her fears and stress aside and got the job done. We are all capable of it, it's the worrying and stressing about things that haven't happened yet that slow us down and affect us but when shit actually hits the fan, we, as humans, deal with it. We're resilient; we move forward by going through it.

Having said all of this, nothing really comes close to real, scary, extremely stressful moments we can face in life. I'm talking about real fear. The kind where you feel like there's no way out.

You've lost your job and don't know how you're going to pay rent. A family member is sick and you feel useless. You're juggling a thousand things and can't stop. That feeling of being in quicksand, desperately trying to come up for air but still sinking. It's scary. And I don't have quick or easy answers ready for you when that happens.

What I will say is that stress is useless. Not once has it helped solve any problem I have come across in my life. It actually makes it worse because it clouds judgement, makes everything messy, rushed and painful. This doesn't mean I won't stress – I'm still human. But it helps to remind myself that worrying about things will only hinder the situation.

And, actually, isn't there usually a way out? I like to believe there is a solution to every problem. I'm an optimist in that sense. Again, doesn't mean I won't stress, but I'll try and find a way out. Stress just makes it a little harder because it fogs your brain. However, if you manage to squash it, suddenly things become lighter in your mind and you can be ready to face any challenge with a clear head. Having perspective and being able to take a step back is also key. She says, having just told us about that motorway fiasco...

I'm not saying at 30 years old I have my shit together. I'm saying I'm *trying*.

I don't know if I'll ever get rid of stress; I don't think it's actually possible. But I think we can learn to coexist with it in a productive way. I like to think we can. Talk to me when I'm late for my flight or I have to perform on stage in front of 400 people. Might be a different story.

The reason I'm bringing this up is, one, to tell you that if you deal with stress as well, you are not alone. We ALL deal with levels of it so give yourself a break. Two, I definitely have progressed in my way of dealing with stress on a day-to-day basis. When you reach 30, it does give you a bit of perspective because you realise that most of your twenties were, in fact, spent worrying about things that don't matter and imagining stupid scenarios in your head. No one has it figured out in their twenties so, in that sense, relief kicks in, and whatever stressed you out in your twenties, simply doesn't anymore. I mean, of course, school is important, but it was definitely not worth the stress it caused me, and I hope you dealt with it better than I did. Because school eventually ends, and no one will die if you get a bad grade. Adult life will put you through more challenging situations, but it doesn't mean you have to let stress control it. It is about letting go of the things you cannot control.

Three, ask yourself simple but useful questions that will help rationalise your thought process. What am I actually worried about? Do I have control over it? How can I fix this? Is anyone dying right now? Asking questions like this will slow you down and make you pay attention to the stuff that matters and can be fixed.

Finally, and this bears repeating, mostly for my sake, stressing out about something that might not happen is a WASTE OF TIME. Don't indulge in it. Don't give any time to it. Be better than me. You can do it. Hell, I can do it! Let's do it together.

Deal With Your Emotions Head-On

Feelings and emotions. It's good to have them. Great, even. I think it means you're not dead inside, which is always a nice, reassuring thought. But if you're anything like me and have become a bit of an expert at shoving some uncomfortable feelings down in the hope they will quietly disappear, well, I'm sorry to say, that method is a sham and ends now.

I'm not going to sugar-coat it, because I'm sure these are things you already know and may not have wanted to hear, but avoiding emotions and feelings is not a solution; it's doomed to fail.

Emotions aren't dumb, either. They are annoyingly smart. Even though they can very well see that you're not paying attention to them, it doesn't mean they will go away. They can sit very comfortably in your body for days, weeks, months even, and won't flinch until you do something about it. They won't leave, but they will become impatient. They'll boil up, which, surprise surprise, leads to stress, anxiety, anger, sadness and many other delightful things that fuck up our day.

What's even more annoying is that this can start very small. It can start with something a friend or family member said that didn't sit quite right with you, but you thought it best to remain silent and brush it off. Suddenly, you're angry, stressed out, over-thinking things and in an unshakeably bad mood for days, when all it might have taken was a conversation to clear the air.

What I've observed over time is that it's important to realise where and how in your life stress comes about. Observe your thought process. Are you an over-thinker, worrying about things that haven't happened yet? Are you upfront with yourself about your feelings? Are you in tune with your emotions? Do you talk about them? What are you scared of? Do you care too much about what people think? Have you found ways to deal with your emotions?

I ask these questions here because in my twenties I never asked them myself. I never spent time assessing what was going on in my head. A lot of my twenties were just spent being lost in a sea of messy, uncontrollable, overwhelming emotions. And I thought that's what being a 20-something was meant to be. I had no clue how to deal with my feelings, and I thought maybe I could outsmart them by crushing them cold when they became too much to handle, which obviously led to situations that could've been avoided if I had paid more attention to how I was feeling, by speaking out loud and asking myself those useful questions asked above.

Don't let your emotions linger inside. Seems like an easy task. It's not, people. But recognising when releasing those emotions from within is needed is a good start. Let whatever needs to come out, *out*. It can be through writing it down, saying it out loud, recording it on your phone, screaming, crying...anything really. Releasing it somehow, in order to create some relief and unburden yourself of those heavy emotions. They will only become heavier and heavier as time goes by, otherwise. Personally, I can live in denial about my stressful thoughts and feelings for a long time. I'm an expert at that.

A friend might say to me, 'Oh, you seem a bit stressed today, what's up?' and I'll usually reply something along the lines of: 'What are you talking about? I'm fine. I'm super busy at work, which is great, waiting to hear about this important casting. I've got a wedding to attend and a paper to write. So-and-So hasn't messaged in a week but I'm sure he's just busy too. I'm feeling great. Just got a lot on my plate, blah blah blah.' I'll pile so much on in my life, try and juggle many things and play this Deny You're Overstretching Yourself Game for a long while, until insomnia, heart palpitations, headaches and stomach cramps kick in.

It's very easy to avoid dealing with your feelings, absurdly easy in fact. We all do it. We all have fast-paced, busy lives where multi-tasking is just part of the game and at times, we think dealing with sadness, frustration, anger, and disappointment can be something for next month. But similar to our body's way of poking us (as described in the Being Kind To Your Body chapter), I can assure you, your mental state can also pack a punch or two. If you let your feelings, fears, and stressful thoughts sit in your head too long, they will absolutely burst out, usually at the wrong time in a big dramatic, possibly inappropriate way.

Case in point: a few years ago, I broke up with a guy. It was fairly amicable. The relationship was just not working and that was that. But I decided to not actually *deal* with it. What I mean by that is I was pretending like nothing sad or disappointing had happened and shoved down every feeling I had for a couple of weeks afterwards. One day, I woke up feeling so tense and I could not shake it off. My neck, my head, and my whole body were like a rock. I couldn't understand why, and it got me even more frustrated and stressed. In the afternoon, I had to go to a casting for a KitKat commercial. *Very similar to when an ex texts you just when your life is back on track, casting directors decide to call you in for the most cheerful casting ever when they sense your life is utter crap.* I managed to drag myself to this casting, which was in Soho. I sat in the waiting room, still feeling this completely blocked-in tension, and very much looking forward to the whole thing being over.

Another actress in the waiting room recognised me from somewhere. *Probably from one of the ridiculously high numbers of castings I've had in my lifetime.* She sat next to me and as she was chatting away, she suddenly said, 'Oh, hey, how are things going with Dude Who Will Not Be Named?' It was like being smacked in the face with a baseball bat. It sent an electric shock down my spine and all the feelings I had tried so hard to ignore and avoid all came rushing in at once. I started sobbing. Uncontrollably so. In a casting waiting room, surrounded by actors. One of them even handed me a tissue. Enough said. I was mortified but not entirely surprised. I knew perfectly well that I hadn't been dealing with the break-up at all and had clearly misjudged what I felt about it. The break-up itself wasn't bad and had I dealt with its ending way sooner and I would have avoided this dramatic, useless scene. I knew that avoiding it wasn't really a solution, but my pride had taken a hit and I wanted to ignore it for as long as possible.

What I didn't know is that these feelings would manifest themselves in the middle of a casting and disrupt my work life in such a ridiculous way. *You can imagine the casting people were thrilled when they saw my red puffy face as I walked into the room and tried to eat a KitKat in a cheerful, uplifting manner. Safe to say, I didn't get the job.* What was interesting is after that momentary mini-meltdown, the tension in my neck and head disappeared. It released itself along with my pent-up emotions. To my surprise, I felt this huge sense of relief. If only I had figured out how to deal with it sooner instead of crying in a public waiting room...Lesson learnt. The moral of the story is: deal with the feelings NOW and never underestimate the power of a good cry. It can do wonders for your body and mind.

And if crying doesn't do the trick, find other ways to release that stressed-out energy you might be carrying around. Boxing, maybe? Screaming into a pillow? Get creative with it! No judgement here; whatever you have to do to feel better, do it. If it keeps you from crying in inappropriate public places,

I'm right there with you.

You just have to learn to deal with all the unresolved feelings HEAD ON. It might mean having some tough conversations with people, sitting down and taking in that rejection, writing everything down in a journal, or crying over a disappointment while listening to the Songs-That-Make-People-Cry playlist. All of which I have done by the way. *I think the actual playlist was called Cry Your Eyes Out Until Nothing Is Left.*

I had to learn all this the hard way. I mean, listen, as an actress, I get rejected pretty much on a weekly basis. You'd be amazed how easily I take rejection nowadays; I like to think it's a skill. The rejections brush past me. Most of the time at least... Sometimes, it takes just that extra 'No' from a casting director, and suddenly all those knock-backs that I hadn't dealt with, or didn't want to let have an impact on me, come crashing down on me like a sack of spuds.

When that extra 'No' happened, I felt very bruised for a few weeks. I had become so accustomed to brushing the rejections off and trying to move on as quickly as possible that I never let myself even five minutes of being sad or disappointed about it – which is all you really have to do. Give yourself some time to sit with it and *then* you move on. Otherwise, every single thing catches up with you all at once and that is not a pleasant experience, let me tell you.

I have learned to apply this stuff to my life. Just the other week I had a very disappointing rejection from a meeting I was really, truly hopeful about. Instead of doing what I would've usually done, which is ignore it, have a drink and move on, I sat with it the next day. I let myself be sad, mad and upset about it for a few hours. And giving myself that time made it so much easier to move on and be optimistic about the week ahead. If I hadn't done that, I would've been moping around, feeling sorry for myself, keeping all that emotion in for weeks on end.

Let it out, people! If it needs to be let out, LET IT.

I know it's easy to say that talking about our feelings is what's best for us. And there are always going to be parts of our lives that are more difficult to face; some areas of our lives are best left untouched. Others might need to be opened up in order to help us close old chapters and let new, exciting and fulfilling ones take their place. I'm pretty sure that's how you become a happier, more fulfilled, complete person.

I definitely still have some unresolved issues with 'someone'. The list of things that bother me is now becoming very long. I'm not going to lie. It's a long list of subjects I will need to discuss at some point. Am I ready for it? Probably not. How do I know I'm not? Well, I did try to broach it with this person once and we ended up not speaking for a year after that.

For this to work, though, two people have to be willing to talk things through and be in the same place mentally. And this particular person was very adamant that they hadn't done anything wrong to me in the past. Sometimes, people aren't ready to have that conversation with you and you just have to be patient and try to be the bigger person. Not all feelings are meant to be dealt with immediately; it really depends on what you think is best and right for you at the time. Just listen and pay attention to what feels good for you.

Long story short: you shouldn't keep everything bottled up. It's no way to live. Not only is dealing with your emotions going to benefit you in the short term, but you can also utilise those feelings in a healthy, non-damaging manner that will automatically help long-term. It's healing.

And if none of this stuff resonates in any way, let me put it this way:

Ultimately, the goal is to be happy, right? How do you think that's going to be possible if you have a bunch of unresolved feelings stuck in your brain? It can really get in the way of your growth and fulfilment. It clouds everything. Why not try everything possible to minimise the stress in your life?

That's why confronting your feelings is key. It can only help you move forward and live a more peaceful life. Later on in this chapter, I'll discuss some tools that can help in letting stuff out and being at peace with yourself, which includes accepting our faults.

So, *deal* with your shit, because it will, without a doubt, come and bite you if you don't. It will be for the better, trust me.

Crossing Paths With Anxiety

Anxiety does share some similarities with stress but, overall, I would say it's quite a different beast. This is something I only discovered when real anxiety entered my life.

Google's definition is pretty accurate: Anxiety is an emotion characterised by feelings of tension, worried thoughts and physical changes like increased blood pressure.

But it doesn't really touch on how dark and consuming anxiety can be.

I guess when you are quite a stressed-out person to begin with, it is less of a surprise to encounter anxiety at some point in your life. I was 28 when I started having panic attacks. That's 28 years of having absolutely no idea what panic attacks even were.

I had no clue what was happening. All I knew is that, one night, before I was about to fall asleep, I started having heart palpitations and trouble breathing. Out of nowhere. As the firm hypochondriac that I am, I was certain I was having a heart attack. And, of course, the more I worried about it, the worse it got. I didn't sleep that night. For a week or so, the heart palpitations would come and go, really disrupting my sleep, and making me seriously worried. On top of these heart problems, my neck and head were agonisingly tensed-up, and I felt dizzy and nauseous all the time. I couldn't shake off any of these symptoms. After living with this for over a few weeks, I finally cracked and booked an appointment with my GP. I obviously thought this was either going to be some sort of heart defect, a stomach problem or a brain tumour. *I'm all about the drama, guys.* Anxiety never even entered my mind; I knew nothing about it. What I did know is that having no idea what was going on made me panic even more. I really couldn't calm down.

When I arrived at the doctor's, I was very overwhelmed. I had made a mental list of all the problems I could potentially have and was expecting the doctor to confirm my theories. I went in and frantically explained what was going on. I was shaking. The doctor checked my pulse and it was racing. Now, it's important to mention that this doctor knows me really well. I have blood tests done every few months; I go in with random concerns about why my head hurts, why I have an eye twitch or why I have a spot there, and could we have an x-ray scan done for my stomach as I'm feeling something weird here? Oh, don't give me that look. I'm fully aware I am nuts and irrational when it comes to my health, and so is he, but he goes along with it! Mostly because he knows it's the only way to get rid of me.

So, even though a young woman with a racing pulse wasn't great, he also knew me well enough and had a strong inkling that anxiety had crept up on me, big time. He didn't say those exact words of course. To calm me down, he suggested I carry a heart monitor for 48 hours and get some blood tests done. My favourite! The thing you need to know about me, when it comes to my health, is that I need to see things on paper, in black and white. I needed proof that nothing was physically wrong with me for me to believe what the doctor had to say, which is why he ordered all those tests to begin with. I really don't know why he keeps putting up with my crap.

After all my disaster scenarios, the tests came back completely normal and I was reassured that those tension headaches were not a brain tumour. The doctor explained that the heart palpitations were in fact panic attacks and that they were a symptom of anxiety. I was confused. How could anxiety give me such strong physical issues that disrupted my daily life and consumed my thoughts 24/7? And without any warning – how rude!

Truth is, anxiety sneaks up on you. It's the culmination of being a stressed person to begin with but also stems from lifestyle, genetics, food habits, environment, sleep patterns, mental health, screen time, breathing and so on. It's usually a combination of all these things. And if just one of them deviates off course, it can trigger a tremendous amount of anxiety – if you let it.

Having panic attacks can feel like the world is ending, that your heart is giving up, that there's no way out. The darkness seems never-ending. I should know: I sometimes find myself at 4 am, pacing in my room, trying to find ways to stop my over-thinking brain. It feels awful, just awful.

Now, the good news is, that feeling is TEMPORARY. It does not last. You might think it does when you're in it but trust me, it will go away. There is a way out and you'll be stronger for it. Unfortunately, to get out of it, you have to go through it.

I remember when I was younger, and I had a dentist appointment. I went into the office feeling already quite nervous. Funnily enough, I'm not a huge fan of someone drilling into my teeth. I got to the reception, not feeling great, and the receptionist was extremely rude and frankly quite mean. She told me to go sit and wait. While I was sitting there, I could feel it coming – that horrible, uncontrollable feeling of panic, rising into my body, reaching my head and everything started spinning. I began to sweat and black spots blurred my vision. My heart was racing and I turned to my mum, who thankfully was there, and knew what was happening. She put my head between my legs and fetched some cold water to put on the nape of my neck. I was so embarrassed. I had no control over my anxiety, and it made me really angry and frustrated. You can imagine how deeply upsetting this would have been for a control freak. I did manage to get through the appointment. I went home and said to Mum: 'This really is not supposed to be this hard. Sitting in a dentist's waiting room should not be that painful. What the F is going on?'

Since then, I made the decision to really work on myself, to find ways to make life easier and happier. Isn't that the whole point? It all comes down to your thoughts and how you process them.

First things first: Don't believe every thought you have. Don't let your thoughts consume you. Observe them, select the useful ones and put aside the ones that are just insults to yourself on repeat. A trick I use is that I picture my thoughts as a rolling film in front of me and I select the ones I really want to see happen and what will benefit me. If you observe and look into yourself, you'll know where and when the triggers are, and you'll figure out the tools to deal with them.

Anxiety doesn't go away on its own, but the good news is it can be more manageable if you figure out ways to tame it, by doing things that work for you. For example, one thing that triggers my anxiety and stress levels is the fact that I'm a hypochondriac. A headache, stomach pain or a weird-looking mole and I'm anxiety's golden patient. So, in this instance, I know that Googling my symptoms won't help in any way. I'll just spiral and lose an hour obsessing about the WebMD page that told me I had 30 days to live. Unhelpful. I simply refuse to be dragged into that cycle anymore. And breaking it helps manage the anxiety.

I can feel overwhelmed when I know I have a lot to juggle, and a lot of things to get done. What helps me is making lists and ticking things off those lists. It's a small thing but it helps me visually see what I am getting done; crossing something out feels like things are moving forward at that moment.

Asking myself: 'Ok, so at this moment in time, what can you control and what is actually out of your hands?' And then telling myself: 'Let go of the things that are out of your control' helps me to define what I can do in any given moment of anxiety and what I have to let go of and leave up to the world.

Any little thing that can help you alleviate stress and anxiety is valid. Finding those tools takes time and practice and sometimes you will fail. Sometimes, the sense of dread overwhelms you and that pain in your stomach doesn't go away so easily; it sits tightly in your core and hurts. Shaking it off is easier said than done, it can feel impossible and endless. However, I'm here to tell you that you CAN do it. It might take a minute, days or even weeks, but it will pass once you find ways to make that happen for yourself.

I remember one year being so consumed by all this anxiety and stress that one of my friends suggested I go see a Reiki healer. Now, I'm quite a cynical person and was really not inspired by the idea. However, my headaches were getting worse and the tension in my heart was constant; I was exhausted. So, I agreed to a session and it was the best thing I could've done for myself. This woman immediately called out all my symptoms, one by one. She taught me about energy, vibrations, breathing and being grounded.

What is important to understand is that when you have anxiety, it's usually because of your thought process, your hyperactive mind, worries and fears, but also because you believe every thought you have.

All that nervous energy gets stuck and consumes your entire headspace. Energy works much better when it is spread throughout your body and grounding this energy is something I learned during that session. The healer sat me down on a chair opposite her and we closed our eyes. Encouraging me to pretend that weights were pulling me to the floor helped ground my energy. After a few minutes, my head felt as light as a feather. All that nervous energy had been projected into the ground. Everything was clear and bright; the headaches were gone.

We then proceeded to do a Reiki session which involved lying down for an hour while she healed parts of my body she felt needed to be healed and worked on. I left feeling a huge weight off my shoulders and just so relieved.

I couldn't believe that after weeks of tension, pain and constant headaches, all of it was gone. I felt reinvigorated, light and full of balanced energy floating through me. 'Balance' being the key word. That's what is important here. Balancing out the energy in us, making sure it is equally measured everywhere. It makes us feel aligned and closer to who we are meant to be. In short, it was quite magical.

I'm not saying you have to necessarily go and see someone like this to fix your problems with anxiety, but I do think it's essential to learn more about anxiety and figure out its meaning and where it's coming from. If you figure out the 'where and the why', you can proceed to the 'how to fix it' part. And I can tell you, going from how to fix it to actually fixing it is pretty much the best part of the whole process. Finding the tools to work with yourself, instead of against yourself, will make you feel stronger than ever, and you will carry that strength in everything you do. I certainly do.

It doesn't happen overnight but once you've figured out that anxiety can be managed and even, dare I say it, squashed, a big weight will be lifted and you will embrace the tools that helped you get there. That's where we are heading next.

Meditation and Breathing

Everyone has different ways of dealing with their issues. This is coming from my personal experience, nothing else.

Recognising you have a problem is step one, figuring out the causes of your troubles is step two, and finally finding the tools to fix it and finding peace along with them, is the end game. Balancing out your energy is key, but it has to be learned.

In comes meditation. I *knooow*, I used to roll my eyes and completely tune out when people kept going on about it, too. What is so great about sitting in silence and listening to your own breath?! I didn't get it. I didn't even *try* to get it for a very long while. But I really wish I had taken that advice when I was in my early twenties; it would've saved me a few years of unnecessary panic attacks and endless visits to the doctor.

What made me finally say yes to meditation? A combination of actually wanting the anxiety to stop, some great people around me inspiring me to try it, many great reads that I thoroughly recommend (see Aunty Ange tips), lovely Fernanda – my reiki healer, and countless videos on YouTube.

I was beginning to understand that everything starts with meditation and when you think about it, it really is not a big ask to sit down in silence and breathe for 5, 10, or 30 minutes a day.

Meditating seems impossible at first because we have busy lives and we are experts at making excuses. Not to mention that muting your thoughts is bloody hard. This is why you start with baby steps. I started meditating for five minutes a day – usually in the morning. I used to think of it as the length of a good song and that would relax me into doing it. Surely I could sit still for the length of a George Michael song? How hard could it be?

At first, I felt like it was a waste of time. Nothing was happening. There was no epiphany, no calm. I was thinking about my day, the emails I had to reply to, the to-do list that was not even close to being ticked off, the lack of work, the bills to pay, my purpose in life, etc. My thoughts were LOUD. Really loud. I didn't realise how loud they had become until I sat on the floor for five minutes and saw them go absolutely mad in my brain. It was like watching a bunch of strings tangle themselves up into a massive knot. I took it as a sign that I really needed this meditation. I needed to give it a chance. Even though I was reluctant, the wanting to calm my brain down was stronger.

Someone had once told me that if you do something for 21 days straight, it becomes a habit and part of your daily life without much effort.

So, I made it a goal to do this for 30 days and see what happens. *Because I'm a show-off and if I can do 21 days, I can also do 30 days.*

Well, let me tell you. By day 20, not only was I enjoying those five minutes of peace and quiet, I had actually extended my meditation to 15 minutes! Every morning, I looked forward to that little bit of time fully devoted to myself and my wellbeing. Regardless of what sort of day lay ahead, if I had allowed myself that time, I knew it would improve my day massively.

Of course, some days my thoughts were still very loud, but I developed a few techniques. Every time a thought popped into my head, I would picture a huge sound speaker in front of me, and I'd imagine turning the button way down until it muted the sound. Other times, when I would catch myself thinking random thoughts, I would just say out loud 'Thinking' until it stopped. Another thing that proved successful was imagining balloons flying out of my head, each balloon carrying a thought with it, far, far away. Little tricks. *I'd like to know what yours are.*

There is something really special about sitting in silence, with yourself, fully present and not thinking about anything but that moment. Most of the time, while meditating, I imagine a big bright circle surrounding me, protecting me from everything else out there. It's my safe space.

You might not be able to control what goes on out there, but in your meditation bubble, you are completely safe. Nothing can touch you there. Isn't it amazing to think such a space exists? No matter how shitty the week has been – maybe you've received some bad news, or nothing seems to be going to plan – if you meditate and manage to shut the noise out and focus on just that present moment, sitting on the floor, you will feel more energised and invigorated than if you hadn't allowed yourself those five minutes. I promise. Nothing is more important than allowing yourself that time of peace, rest and escape. In that bubble, it's all enough.

Slowly but surely, I went from meditating five minutes a day to 25 minutes a day, sometimes meditating twice if something was overwhelming me. I've used many brilliant guided meditations online (see Aunty Ange tips) to help me get to those 25 minutes, without feeling like it was a lifetime. *And believe me, two years ago, 25 minutes of meditation would've felt like a painful LIFETIME to me.*

Meditation does not require anything else but yourself. And it's FREE. It's the one thing you can do anywhere, anytime you need to. It's for you. It's self-care. Even on the days when you feel a bit sorry for yourself, do it. Simply because, whatever you do for the rest of the day, you at least know you've done that one thing for you and only you. And that's progress. It's huge.

If you are still resisting this, *like I was a few years ago, thinking 'Oh here we go, it's the meditation speech again',* let me put it like this: You have a choice of going one of two ways here. You can spiral out of control in a sea of bad thoughts and self-deprecation OR you can sit on the goddamn floor of your room, close your eyes and *decide* to make all those thoughts, fears, and worries stop and maybe, just maybe, open the door to a world of endless possibilities and goals. What's more appealing to you?

YOU have the ability to shut all that noise and create something better for yourself. That's the beauty of meditation that I didn't know about. Not only does it feel great to make those thoughts stop for a moment, but when you manage to silence your brain, amazing things take place. A brilliant idea will pop up, a new goal will arise, and inner peace will extend itself throughout the day. And what happens then? What happens when you feel good about yourself, and you feel hopeful and limitless in your abilities? Well, you suddenly attract goodness. People respond to that; they are inspired by that and will be drawn to you, will want to help you, and that's when amazing things start happening. All because you sat down on the floor every day for a few minutes and silenced that useless noise. If you meditate every day, you will immediately start seeing those benefits in your own life because you'll become more in tune with yourself, with those around you, and this will automatically attract better things. And why wouldn't you want to attract better things?

Not only will it reduce your stress levels, but it'll also bring more exciting things into your life, things that you could've never imagined before because you've finally let your brain *breathe* for a second. It really is that simple and it's a freakin' godsend! *Except God didn't bring this to your attention, I did. Not to toot my own horn or anything...*

Speaking of breathing. Just do it. BREATHE. It's literally the first thing we do in life and yet we take it very much for granted. The biggest moments in life, the most stressful situations, and the scary times are helped if you just take a flippin' deep breath. Trust me on this one.

Meditation and breathing definitely go hand-in-hand. The more you meditate, the more attention you place on your breath. Taking a deep breath will also make you realise that you are still alive, you're still there. As long as you're breathing, you will be OK.

So just remember, when you feel overwhelmed or when something bad happens, if you can find it in you, to force a deep breath, the results can be immediate. You're taking back control of your emotions by slowing your breathing down. When you do that, things become clearer, solutions will arise; it gives you more perspective instead of letting your emotions run wild.

The same applies when you're angry or upset and you're about to react as quickly as paper burning; try to stop yourself and take that deep breath. Of course, if you still feel like yelling after a few deep breaths, then please, be my guest. I've been known to do just that from time to time, and it feels good. But I would say, most of the time, in order to assess a situation, use your breath. That's what it's there for. *Along with, you know, keeping you alive.*

All of this took me some time to implement in my daily life. Most of my twenties were NOT about breathing and finding my zen time, quite the opposite. So, there is no timeframe on this. You do it in your own time, when it feels necessary for you to do so. And please don't be so hard on yourself. I definitely have weeks when meditating, breathing and staying calm is just not going to happen. *My mood can be pretty stubborn sometimes.* But I learn to sit with that, forgive myself and know that tomorrow will be better. Storms do pass. They might bring some doom and gloom for a minute, but they do go away, and it will be OK. And honestly, if a stress ball and over-thinker like me can embrace meditation, I have no doubt there is hope for any of you struggling with all the 'gems' anxiety and stress offer.

You are also allowed to *not* embrace meditation at all and find other avenues to help you navigate anxiety in your life. That is absolutely valid, too.

Meditation is just what has worked for me. But before you say no to it, just try it. Do it for yourself. And for me. Give it a shot, you'll make me so happy. *I know we don't know each other at all, but if you do give meditation a try, just imagine a small mess of a woman smiling somewhere in London, really proud of you right now. Maybe I even have a single tear running down my cheek... Too much? OK, but really, WELL DONE.*

And here is a little reassuring reminder; if you get stressed about feeling like you have no clue what's going on or what you're doing with your life. Stop that now. NO ONE has a clue. Not a single soul knows what they are doing. And if they seem like they do, I promise you they are lying or they have some other shit they are dealing with. Everyone has their demons to fight. Do not stress about thinking you need to figure out life. It's a waste of time. Trying to figure out life is like trying to figure out how planes fly. Don't question it, just accept that it's happening and try to enjoy the ride.

Life isn't supposed to be easy, but it's supposed to be lived to the best of your ability. You have the means to choose to find happiness and healing for yourself. Why not give it a try? Anxiety, stress, fears and worries can be navigated. They are not permanent and don't have to be a barrier to your happiness. Choose to do something about them. Don't let them step all over you. Tackle them head-on. Use them to be stronger. Fight them so you can tell your story. And who knows, maybe by doing all that work on yourself, you'll help someone else in the process. *Wink wink.*

AUNTY ANGE TIPS

Here are some tips, to relieve some of that stress, that I've learned on the rollercoaster of emotions I've been through and still go through to this day:

- Cry. We've covered this one but it's one of my favourites, so I'll reiterate. A good cry is never a waste; the uglier the better. Let all those nerves go and really go for it. I want to see tears. I want to see puffy eyes. And then you can reward yourself with ice cream. Win-win. And if you happen to make a killer 'Crying' playlist that you're proud of, don't be selfish, send it my way.

- Meditate. I won't go on about this longer than I already have. You know the drill. Do it, or at least try. If not for you, do it for me. Guided meditations and uplifting videos on YouTube include, *The Honest Guys, Rising Higher Meditation, Oprah's SuperSoul Conversations, Jim Carrey and Chadwick Boseman's graduation speeches* cheer me right up, *The Mindful Movement, Abraham Hicks videos, Gabrielle Berstein,* to name a few.

- Cook. Now, this is definitely not a favourite of mine, since I'm useless at it, but I have been told it helps with stress. For some, it is soothing, occupying the hands and brain for a while. And, as a bonus, you hopefully get a nice meal out of it.

- Iron. This is a weird one, but it has happened to calm me down more than once. Do the ironing. Yes, you heard me. Don't ask me why, but ironing clothes can be really soothing. I'll either listen to music while doing it or put a TV show on. I think it might be the combination of using my hands and seeing my messy clothes become smooth again. I don't know, but it works. I wish I could say the same with hoovering or making the bed but at least it's one chore I enjoy.

- Knit. My best friend tells me she knits when she's stressed or worried. It's another simple, hands-on activity option. Plus, you get homemade winter accessories. Jackpot.

- Draw. I find this to be a nice escape. All you have to do is pick up a pencil and paper and draw whatever comes to mind. Drawing can be calming. It can stir up the creative side of the brain, which is always more joyful and positive. It is for me, at least! I happen to come up with great ideas or solutions while drawing, and that's always a nice surprise. How about giving it a try and seeing what happens?

- Exercise your brain and take your mind off things with mindless activities; crossword puzzles or actual puzzles, for example. They don't hurt. Find your thing that busies the mind and run with it.

- Listen to music and podcasts. They are a wonderful way to escape and calm oneself. And there is always something for everyone and for every mood.

- Try acupuncture. This is something I tried recently and responded to really well. I know the idea of needles in the body isn't appealing to many people but in some weird way, I left every session feeling more relaxed and energised than ever. Worth a shot!

- Get a massage. Don't need a reason for this one. Treat yourself.

- Read. Books have helped me through some tough times. Here are a few: *The Power of Now* by Eckhart Tolle, *You Are a Badass*' by Jcn Sincero, *Eat, Pray, Love* by Elizabeth Gilbert, *Ask And It's Given*' by Ester and Jerry Hicks, *Untamed* by Glennon Doyle, *WE* by Gillian Anderson and Jennifer Nadal, *The Seven Laws of Success* by Deepak Chopra.

- Talk to someone. Either a close friend or, if you have the means, a therapist. Sometimes, someone from outside your life, who has no idea who you are, is the best person to advise you on how to manage your anxiety and help you find a way out of it. This idea that there is shame around talking to a qualified professional is absolute bullshit. Do not ever feel ashamed for going to see a therapist. I genuinely think everyone would benefit from talking to a shrink. Regardless of who you talk to, it's important to let it out and share what you're going through. Everyone is going through something; let's help each other out.

VII. YOUR INSTINCTS, USE THEM

Choices and decisions. Life in a nutshell. Don't you ever wish someone could make your life decisions for you?! *Ugh, wouldn't that be a cool...though exhausting, job?*

It's no picnic, guys. When we're kids and teenagers, we're not really prepped for how many choices we're going to have to make in our lifetime. The number of times we're going to be deciding stuff about how our life is going to go. No one gave us even an inkling of what that looks like. And then, boom. You're in your twenties, and you are faced with a tremendous amount of overwhelming choices that feel larger than life.

It's just a fact. We are, without a doubt, going to encounter many different, possibly challenging, situations where choices will have to be made. Some choices will be obvious to us, others will be quite difficult and complex to navigate through, especially if we want to stay true to who we are.

Now, we've already been through this but let's reiterate: Who you are and who you *think* you are can get a little blurry at times, simply because people might influence your decisions and those outer voices can cloud your judgement. Circumstances can change. Maybe even you can change. Those years do test your identity and your instincts in a big way. And the same way no one tells you that you're going to be making a shit ton of choices in your life, no one tells you that those life choices are not all going to be the right call. Apparently, that's completely normal...*doesn't make it any less stressful, though!* However, the good news is, with age, learning to trust your gut, value your instincts, know your worth, cut out the toxicity around you and really apply those strong instincts in your life, everything gets a little easier and doubts about what choices you're meant to make and what path you're supposed to follow become a little less scary.

Your instincts and that gut feeling are what is going to get you through your twenties and they need to be paid attention to. Obviously, I'm not saying your instincts are always going to be right, but trusting yourself will help build confidence and self-assurance that you *are* on the right track. And even if you feel you really aren't on the right track, I promise you that you are closer to being right than wrong. You just have to lean into the process and trust it.

Trust Your Gut

Let's start with that famous gut feeling. And no, I'm not talking about the various never-ending stomach issues we face nowadays. *I wanna find the person who isn't bloated right now and congratulate them.* No, I'm talking about the other gut feeling. We all know what it means but sometimes, *a lot of the time,* we either don't know what it actually is, we don't pay attention to it or we choose to ignore it.

If I had a pound for every time someone told me 'What is your gut telling you' or 'Just go with your gut, trust it', I would be very rich. And half the time I would frustratingly tell them: 'But I don't know what my bloody gut is telling me, YOU tell me what to do!'

Over time, however, as you get to know yourself a bit more and discover what's best for you, that gut feeling grows stronger. You also learn that only YOU know what's best for you. People can certainly advise you but ultimately you're in charge of your life. You call the shots. And, even though my saying this doesn't cancel out the amount of times I wish people could've just told me what to do and explain what was best for me, I have learnt to figure out what the right thing for me is...*cough cough, most of the time.*

As you already know, I am an actress. *Whoopdeedoo! Can she shut up about it already?* In the tiny town in Brittany where I come from, most people's ambitions were teaching, bartending, working as a sales manager in a shoe shop, getting married, buying a house or becoming a parent. Nothing wrong with any of those things at all but, from an early age, I knew I wanted something different from my life. I wanted to act, I wanted to travel, I wanted to work with people from all over the world. But when you're 12, and no one has any of the same aspirations, you start thinking 'Ok, maybe I should do what everyone else is doing; it seems like the safest thing to do and it'll be much easier than trying to pursue acting in London...' I certainly could have chosen to follow that voice and that path, but I just knew it wasn't going to make me happy or fulfil me in any way. Even at that age, I knew I wanted more.

I remember one day in class, when I was 13, the teacher asked us to write down on a piece of paper what we wanted to do when we grow up. I wrote down: 'I want to be an actress and travel the world.' The papers were anonymous and we put them all in a hat. At the end of the school year, the teacher read the papers out loud to the class to see if we still wanted the same things. When he read my paper outloud, the whole class laughed. I remember him calming the class down and saying 'Well, whoever this is, I hope it comes true.' He looked at me and gave me a wink. He had guessed it was me, and I still remember that moment. It was so encouraging and kind. Instead of focusing on the entire class laughing and mocking the idea, that one person made me believe it was possible. My gut feeling grew stronger that day. I just knew this was the right path for me and I trusted that. This does not mean I didn't have serious doubts after that or that it always worked out every time I trusted my gut, *hell no,* but for this particular choice, I wasn't wrong.

Having fearless people around you, who are examples of what making bold, gut-led choices looks like, helps. My mum, who I realise is featuring a lot in this book – *and rightfully so, she is one of a kind* – was instrumental in showing me how trusting your instinct, even when you can't really explain why, works out. After her divorce from my dad, we had to move out of the house in Belgium that we were living in. Mum was looking for a house to buy and everyone in her life was pushing her to stay in Belgium. She decided to go for a little holiday on her own, to my grandma's house in Brittany, to clear her head. When she came back, she knew that what was best for her, at that time, was to move back to France and be closer to her family. Now, that is a big move, right? Moving countries with two kids and no job prospects in sight was bold and risky. And yet she ignored all those outside voices and listened to her own. She couldn't explain why but she just knew it was what was best for her and what would make her happier. And it worked out pretty well. She got her dream house, five minutes from the beach, found a job in a school, and is much closer to her mother and her sisters now than she ever was before. It also meant that my brother and I got to grow up in Brittany and immerse ourselves in French culture, our own heritage. She trusted her gut and if you ask her today, she would say she does not regret that decision at all. *Unless she's lying to me and I need to have a more in-depth conversation with her later.*

What she taught me here, too, is that people will always have opinions about you and how they think you should live your life. It's going to happen no matter what. You have to choose the voices you're going to take on board and the ones you're going to ignore.

But here's a thing I wish I had known early on – *it would've saved me years of feeling sorry for myself and cursing my life choices over and over again*: going with your instincts does not mean you are always going to get it right. You're not. You're not always going to pick the right thing. It's just how it is. No one is perfect and no one can 100 percent know all the time what's right for themselves. Do you know how many times I've moved into a new flat thinking it was a great move and then six months later hating everything about the area, the people I was living with and the room? Or that time I thought being the lead role in a cool indie film, *that no one saw*, was better than a commercial? Or when I went to America for the first time, thinking it would be my big break, to find out three months later that being in LA without a driver's licence, money or a fucking clue was maybe not the best career move of all time? *I also found out that the house I was sharing with seven people in Santa Monica got repossessed six months after I left...apparently, there was a meth lab in the basement. Very Hollywood.*

It also doesn't mean those choices are going to be useless or a waste of time. On the contrary. Those mistakes and mishaps were vital for my own growth and life experience. I just had to go down a few bad routes in order to know what was right for me. Life lessons! I learned that if you're waiting at a bus stop in LA for a bit too long, people will mistake you for a prostitute. I learned that if the rent is cheap in a nice neighbourhood in London, the likelihood of the place turning out to be illegal or a dump is very high. I learned that living with two very loud, unhygienic Italian football fans is never going to be a long-term situation. Two months tops. I learned that indie films are great, but that doing the research on the team who is making the film is kind of the main f***ing thing I needed to do before agreeing to the job and turning down a Pringles commercial that would've paid my rent for three months. Endless lessons, guys. But you live and learn. Literally.

And that goes for all areas of your life: from studies and career choices to friendships and relationships. All of it happens for a reason. All of those mistakes led you to the path you are on now, which is the one you are meant to be on. You can 100 percent trust that. *Which doesn't mean it doesn't suck for a minute, though, I know.*

In addition to that, there will be, at some point in your life, a time where you're not going to listen to what your gut is telling you. In fact, you'll purposefully avoid it. You know what I'm talking about, right? We humans love a bit of self-sabotage, don't we? Smoking, drinking, doing drugs, having sex with the wrong person, cheating, stealing, staying silent when we know we should speak up or saying something that would've been better kept to oneself. The list is long. I am not saying I've personally done all of these things, although I have definitely made some choices that I knew, deep down, were not going to improve my life at all. But, hey, life is always more interesting with a bit of self-destruction and drama, no? In moderation I'd say... *Joking guys, joking...mostly*. But it is true that most humans, at some point in their lives, will be more attracted to what is wrong. I have spent quite a bit of time wondering why this is. Why are we attracted to the bad stuff – the stuff we KNOW is not going to end well but we do it anyway? Maybe it's the thrill of it, maybe it's boredom, maybe it's wanting to learn something or it's just a question of being curious, who knows. Everyone has their reasons! There is nothing wrong with exploring what life has to offer, the good and the bad, and maybe you're meant to go through the bad stuff to know what's right for you.

However, making the wrong choices can become quite tedious, repetitive in its outcome, and I don't know about you, but ultimately at 30 years of age, I don't want to repeat past mistakes. It's exhausting and unfulfilling. I want to grow and see what happens when I listen to that voice inside that is screaming: 'Oh hell no, you're NOT choosing this guy again!' or 'That person is making you feel like shit, why are we still letting them do that?' or 'I hate going to work, is that normal?' or 'Weird how that friend always messages when she needs something, what's up with that?' That voice needs to be paid attention to. ASAP.

Now, bad habits are difficult to let go of, because you think they bring you comfort and let's face it, it's so easy to just be lazy and ignore the good voice in you. I'm not saying that having phases of feeling like crap and cutting loose isn't OK, not at all. *I'm often first in line for Let's Do Something Stupid, when I'm in a mood, but more and more, I try to fight against that instinct.* And if, like me, you are at a point in your life where you see the same outcome and you're not happy with it, well that gut feeling will kick in, harder, and you'll have no choice but to stop and reevaluate.

Oh, I forgot to mention that this chapter does not concern the people who have their shit together, always follow their good instincts and only make good decisions in life.

I feel like I also need to put this down in writing: This does not mean I am now immune to making mistakes, OK? I probably will, many many times over. Turning 30 doesn't mean I have it figured out, it just means that instead of repeating the same mistake, I'll find creative ways to make new ones. *Fun times ahead.*

Joking aside, as you grow older you simply learn to go with that gut feeling more often. Give yourself a bit more credit. Trust yourself. Stop second-guessing yourself. And don't be too hard with the mistakes you've made, either. All of it has taken you this far. I'm not worried. And neither should you be.

Of course, they'll be moments of doubt. Moments where you think your gut has screwed you over big time. It's played the worst trick on you. I cannot tell you the number of times, in my twenties, when I was convinced I had made an awful mistake with my choice of career. What the hell was I even thinking, moving to London and ACT for a living? How did I think that being an actress was going to be a good idea? That was pretty much a weekly feeling... for YEARS. The 'Oh no, I've spent seven years in a career that I was never meant to choose and now what do I do? I'm a loser. I've made a terrible mistake – I'm actually a terrible actor. This is not how I envisioned my life at 27. None of my goals have been met, I've achieved nothing, I AM nothing! What does it all mean?'

Sound familiar? It's glorious, isn't it? Rethinking all our life choices is just part of it, guys. No one tells you but it's what happens once in a while.

It doesn't mean your instincts are off, it just means you're paying more attention to the doubtful thoughts than your confident ones. It's OK, we have all been through it.

You just have to regroup, realign and shut the fuck up, *respectfully.* Let the gut feelings take the wheel again. Granted, some choices are more difficult than others and might take a bit longer to make. Some can feel nearly impossible to make and they may not be pleasant and yet, somehow, we make them. We manage. Our instincts are almost never wrong. *Unless, as discussed above, you're just in a phase where self-sabotage is your way of life. No judgement; take your time and come back to us when you are out of it.*

Here's my favourite part, the part my 30-year-old self is very excited to tell you. As you grow older, you enter this No Bullshit Zone where your main priority is going to be doing what is right for you and what makes you happy. This means people's opinions matter less and your instincts kick in more because you won't want to waste time being anything less than who you are. So much of my twenties was not trusting myself enough with my instincts, thinking that maybe my instincts had been wrong and had made a mess of everything. And yet I'm exactly where I am meant to be at 30 and even though I don't have everything figured out, I know that my gut feeling hasn't been wrong. It's proved itself to be quite trustworthy over the years and the only thing that was standing in the way of it, was myself and my doubts about it.

As years go by, we know what makes us happy. And that's the ultimate goal, right? Finding moments of happiness. I like to think our gut feeling is with us on this and guides us towards that goal. And if that's not what your goal is right now, it should be. You are worthy of being happy or at least giving yourself the chance to find what makes you happy. Trust your instincts, they know what's best.

And let me tell you something, plain and simple: if it feels wrong, if it feels forced, if it feels like you're doing this to please others, if it doesn't feel like you, it means it's probably the wrong path to take.

Trust that you have got your own back and that YOU know what is right for you. Trust that.

Know Your Worth

Next one. Know your worth (Also touched upon in the Work chapter).

This is too important of a reminder to not be mentioned less than a few dozen times, simply because your self-worth will probably be challenged at times – mine certainly was. So it is important to remind ourselves sometimes what we are worth. *I'm going down the cheesy route here, try not to cringe too much.* Every single person on this planet is unique and has something to contribute to this world, no matter how big or small. You are valid and important. And don't you dare think otherwise.

What is wonderful, and not to be forgotten, is that you are in charge of your own life and you get to decide what you want to accomplish and what you want to be in this life.

However, along the way, some people, sadly, may try to tarnish or diminish you. They will try to install doubt in your mind, pressure you to go in another direction or persuade you that you might not know what is right for you. Those people will always exist. And that's when knowing that you are worth so much more than people might think you are, comes in very handy.

Building that confidence comes from experience, for sure. And the one thing to retain here is: Don't take what you know you don't deserve. Let me repeat that. Do not comply or agree to something you KNOW you don't deserve. I want that message embedded into your brain. Write on Post-it notes, on the wall, or in your notebook.

It's a well-documented fact that us women have it harder. Therefore, we have to be louder and take more risks. But if you take a stance, if you stand up for something you believe in, you will feel more empowered than ever because you'll have been true to yourself. This applies to all areas of your life. Don't get me wrong, it can be terrifying standing up for oneself, especially if there's something to lose. But isn't it better to take a leap of faith, especially if it comes to your self-worth?

As a woman in the acting industry, I've witnessed a lot of inequality and inappropriate behaviour in the workplace. As a young woman entering the business, I had to learn a few hard lessons and realise that some people will try to take advantage of me. The money aspect of things comes into play (also discussed in the Work chapter). There have certainly been a few moments where I felt I had to stand up for myself, by saying no or walking away, all the while crapping my pants in fear of the consequences. *Not literally, folks, it's not that kind of story.* Negotiating a pay check is certainly one of the sticky things about the film industry, but there are sadly other gloomy sides to the profession which challenged me and my worth a lot more. You might have guessed what that is...

There are many men in powerful jobs, who think they have a right to treat you a certain way, especially if you're a young woman just entering the industry for the first time. One particular experience has stuck with me from those early days, one where, even at the age of 22, I fully upheld my standards, said no and left no room for negotiation.

At the time, I was looking to change agents and in the hundreds of emails I sent out, I got a reply from quite a big agent in London who told me to send over my reel. Nothing suspicious there at all – I was thrilled he had taken an interest in my work. After watching my clips, he asked me for my phone number, saying it would be easier to communicate. I was really excited that such a renowned agent had looked at my work and was interested in me, so I didn't think much of it. A couple of days went by and he started sending me WhatsApp messages, messages in which he complimented me, first, praising my work, then my looks. He made subtle insinuations and comments to see if I was single. The conversation then slipped into what I was doing that week and did I maybe want to grab a drink and discuss this further, etc. I felt more and more nervous and uncomfortable because as much as I didn't want to upset him, I also didn't want to date the guy. I kept diverting the conversation, suggesting maybe a meeting in his office to discuss my career. He very expertly dodged my messages and became quite insistent, to the point where he started sending me photos. Photos of him in his living room, him at the gym. We had gone past the uncomfortable stage and into the 'I need to find a way to get rid of this guy without him ruining my career' stage. I was lucky, though, the most inappropriate photo he sent was one of his bare feet in front of a football match on the TV. Don't ask. *Some people are just bizarre.* I managed to stop all communication with him by lying, saying I had now found a new agent and that we no longer needed to meet. While I shouldn't have been too surprised by this, it's a well-known fact that there are many sleaze bags in the film industry, I was surprised at how casual and normally it began; it just completely sneaked up on me. Luckily, very quickly, I knew what he was after and I was not prepared to give in to any of it for a career move.

I ended up mentioning this story to an actress a few weeks later and she told me that this was actually not an isolated case. The agent had apparently tried the same thing with a few girls recently. I was baffled. He was an established agent with a big client list and yet was trying to lure girls in, making them promises in exchange for something else. What was even worse is that I found out a month later he was engaged and his fiancée was expecting a baby...

I am proud of myself for not letting myself be lured in by empty promises, even those from someone who is, by all accounts, successful. Like I said, if it feels wrong, if it goes against what you stand for, you are more than entitled, even encouraged, to walk the other way. *Cue the Beyoncé music, please.*

Do not be scared to stand up for yourself. You're a fighter and much braver than you think you are. At the end of the day, you make your own choices and it's your life. Do what feels right for you and what makes you feel good about yourself. Ask yourself: If I look back at this situation in 10 years time, am I going to feel proud or am I going to regret not taking a stance when I knew I could?

The same very much applies to your personal relationships and friendships. Pay attention to how you are treated and how you feel with that particular person. Are they deserving of your time? Do they appreciate you for who you are? When you leave their company, do you feel like you've been treated well and listened to? It's important to ask yourself these questions because how you feel matters. They also help you understand what your standards are and what you're worth. Don't let anyone diminish your self-worth. No matter how they justify it. You are worth so much more than feeling undervalued, disrespected, unseen, unheard or undeserving of great things. So stand up for yourself, show up for yourself, because no one else will. You *have* to show up for yourself *as* yourself and try not to let fear control what you want people to see.

Learn how to respect yourself too, and believe that you are deserving of great things. People will treat you with the respect you deserve when you demonstrate it yourself. These aren't obvious, easy tasks by the way. So much self-doubt goes through our minds in our twenties. And at times, you'll let some people step all over you or treat you a certain way and if you let it, you'll start believing that you deserve those treatments.

Ultimately, I've learnt to not let anything into my life that is less than what I deserve. Being able to say no when something didn't feel right or when I knew I deserved better was a big one. Cutting out people who made me feel inferior was another. At whatever stage you may be in your life, if people make you feel like shit, unseen or are simply dishonest, it is not worth your time or energy – and time and energy are two precious things; we have to be selective with who and what we give them to.

You know your worth. You alone can determine when to speak up, cut ties, move on and move forward. And if a few people or things popped up in your mind while reading this chapter, take it as a sign to do something about it. Have a conversation and speak up. Use that beautiful voice, be your own person. You're pretty awesome and the people in your life should make you feel nothing less than that.

Toxic Relationships

Speaking of cutting ties, that's something you might have to come across doing once in a while. It's not something you necessarily see coming and it's certainly not pleasant but sometimes cutting certain people out of our lives has got to be done for our own good. It goes hand-in-hand with Knowing What You Deserve.

Toxic relationships are everywhere. We see them, hear about them, and sometimes even participate in them. 'Toxic' might be a tad extreme, it might not. Regardless of the word you want to use, I think it's safe to say we all encounter, at some point in our lives, someone who has a terrible influence on us, who makes us feel insecure or makes us feel small when we could be big, makes us miserable, makes us change. Whether it's a friend, a romantic partner, a family member or even a stranger.

The second you realise that surrounding yourself only with people who love you, support you and make you feel special, valued and understood is vital for your wellbeing, you will weed out the rest.

That said, it takes time to actually realise how bad some people are for you and how deeply some people affect you negatively. These types of relationships sort of sneak up on you too. They don't just happen overnight. They can go on for years until you realise how insecure and far from yourself you feel when you're around that person. I like to think that I'm a pretty good judge of character. My intuition is usually accurate when it comes to letting people into my life. Especially from my mid-twenties onwards. This doesn't mean it was always the case. And actually, an experience I had as a young girl definitely stuck with me in terms of not allowing people to influence me later on.

When I was around 11 or 12, I started hanging out with this girl in school. No one else really liked her and she didn't have any friends. We were paired up in gym class and, just wanting to be friendly, I decided to invite her to join me at lunch. I just wanted to make her feel included and frankly, I didn't care what other students thought. I had been the new girl in a new school once and I didn't want to let this girl be iced out. We became very close friends and started doing most things together, to the point where it was just us two for a while. It took me some time to notice that all my other friends had slowly taken a step back. I didn't think much of it at the time. This girl and I were getting along and having fun. She was very grunge, different, and I thought she was cool. However, after a few months, some weird things started to make me uncomfortable. She began coming up with weird, risky ideas for us to do. She would go on about how she wanted us to flirt with teachers and go get our belly buttons pierced. She would also talk a lot about the fact that she wanted to run away. She would brag about how she had hitchhiked home after school, had already kissed boys and how she had stolen some stuff from a store one time... Looking back, this girl was just bad news. Except, I was 12 and a very innocent, naive girl who just thought she was cool. I also didn't take much of what she said seriously. It never even occurred to me that I would actually engage with any of these things. But, slowly, she tried to subtly push me to be more like her. 'We should pretend that we are runaway girls and hitchhike somewhere' she would say. At first, I just found it funny but somehow, she convinced me to skip school one day and walk as far as we could, see how far we could get, and start hitchhiking. After walking an hour, she started flagging cars down. A truck driver ended up stopping in front of us, looking dodgy as hell. I started to get quite scared and nervous. This was wrong. It felt wrong and I didn't like what this girl was making me do. I told her I wanted to go back and that there was no way

I was getting in that truck. She got really upset. She told me I was boring and that I should go back on my own. As I walked back to the school alone, I couldn't believe how much of a bad influence this girl had had on me. I was in the middle of nowhere, in the middle of a school day, walking alone – and for what, exactly? I felt so stupid that day and decided it would be the last time anyone would influence me in such a negative way. I never spoke to her again after that. It was a wake-up call. I wasn't going to let this girl run all over me and make decisions for me that felt wrong. I took that experience with me for many years to come.

Those types of relationships can happen at any point in your life. At first, it starts with very subtle situations and words thrown at you. Then, suddenly, you're in the middle of a messy situation wondering how the hell it happened. We also have those people who seem good at first and later on, out of nowhere, with zero warning, turn out to be nut-jobs. There's no preparing for that scenario. It just happens and it's a freak-show. My mum would be the first one to agree with this, *which also proves it can happen at any age. BE ON GUARD, people.*

My mum met a woman in a dance class a few years ago and they hit it off really well. I remember her being really excited about having a friend in the same neighbourhood, with similar interests. After all, it's not easy meeting new, solid friends in your forties and fifties. It became a really great friendship. So great, in fact, that I invited them both over to my flat in London for a few days. The week they spent with me was so much fun, really a blast. We went to parties, food markets, and danced in clubs. Perfect. Until the second-to-last night when it all went to shit, drastically and dramatically.

Mum and I had been invited to my friend's engagement party. It was a very small get-together and a private, invite-only event. Mum's friend had known about this from the beginning of the trip and she also knew she was not on that list of invitees. She was fine with it back when we told her, but suddenly on the actual day, she had asked Mum if she could stay with her because she didn't want to be on her own for a few hours. Mum, rightfully so, didn't want to miss out on this important event and explained that we would only be gone a few hours. Well, let me tell you, this 'friend' went batshit crazy. She started insulting us, calling us selfish and unkind before locking herself in my guest room for the night, like a grounded schoolgirl.

Let me remind you that we were dealing with a 40-something-year-old woman here. It was laughable. The whole thing felt like a prank. But we weren't going to let that spoil our evening. We thought we'd let her blow off whatever steam was coming out of her ass and we warned my flatmate that, should an angry woman pop her head out of the room during the evening, not to be alarmed. We just assumed she was having a 'moment'. So, we went to the party and when we came back, not only had the tension not blown over, this woman had packed her bags and placed them in the entrance with a note that said, 'I'm leaving in the morning'. Mum never heard from the woman again. After nearly two years of friendship. We could not believe it. There was nothing to explain it, really.

The quick and easy lesson here is that some people are just especially great at hiding their insanity.

So, my advice would be to think twice about who you invite into your home, and also look out for the signs. Even the smallest ones. And most importantly, do not stick around if they make you feel like shit. Mum took a hit and she was disappointed. Her friendship was full of great laughs and memories, however, that didn't mean she was going to even remotely try to salvage that friendship. This woman not only went apeshit on me, but she made my mum feel terrible for going to a party she was invited to. People like that will only make you feel small when you should be feeling tall and special. Mum knew that she deserved better than a woman who was going to make her feel guilty about going to a stupid party. No thanks, Karen! *Her name's not actually Karen but you know what I mean...*

Pay attention to how people make you feel. Observe how they treat you and other people around you. And, MOST importantly, stop making excuses for them. You can certainly be kind, understanding, compassionate and forgiving, *to a certain extent,* but do not keep making excuses for people who clearly have a bad agenda. You will notice this by the number of times they say sorry, or the number of times you don't feel good enough around them. It sucks and it is not worth the energy. Trust patterns, not apologies.

People who don't enrich your life, who don't teach you, who don't inspire you or uplift you in any way are not worth the excuses you might keep making for them – no matter what they keep coming up with. Your entourage is meant to make you feel better, and make your life better. If they make it worse, painful and harder, that's your answer. It really is that simple, I'm afraid. Making excuses for people only lasts so long before something bursts.

My aunt has a very complicated relationship with one of her oldest and best friends. One I do not understand but it might resonate with some of you. This is a 20-plus-year friendship. There is a lot of history there, not all good. But in the last few years, I've noticed a pattern in how he treats her. He has become very demanding of her, regardless of what is going on in her life.

She will have to make him a priority and if she doesn't, he treats her like absolute garbage. It's painful to watch. He will insult her, scream at her and make her feel like she's a terrible friend. He will do this and then the week after will come back with apologies, gifts or something very thoughtful and special that will make her feel better for a minute and forget what he trashed her with the week before. I have never met anyone more manipulative than he is with her. Why does she let that happen, you ask? I can't really speak for her, but I can maybe guess, knowing her, that it might be her loyalty to this friendship. An over twenty-year friendship is difficult to cut off, especially if you don't have many friends or live close to people you know. It's a tough call to make. He had also been there for her in trying times and feels like maybe she was his only outlet of emotions. I don't know... But many excuses have been given to this guy and coming from someone who has been observing this from the outside, I simply don't get it.

I don't think you should let anyone suck the light out of you, regardless of how long you've known them, how many times they apologise or how many promises they make. And if you have someone in mind right now, it means you're asking yourself the right questions. Does this person make me feel good? Does this person deserve my time? Does this person help me as much as I have helped them? Am I listened to? Do I feel valued here? Do I feel used? How do I feel around this person? The questions aren't always easy to answer but they need to be considered. It'll help make some tough calls for your own sake. Sifting out the bad is important for your own well-being.

A big one to look out for, and something I learned in my twenties, is to really watch how people react when things are going great in your life and when things go to shit. That will tell a lot about what kind of person they are and what their agenda is towards you. I had a 'friend' who always showed great interest in me when I wasn't doing so well or when I had some bad news in my life. I think she liked being there when things were going better for her. However, when things were great for me, when I booked a gig or when it was going well with a person I was dating, she was nowhere to be found.

Haven't we all encountered those people? You know, those people who check in with you just to see if you still have that great job or maybe they heard it's not going so great with the boyfriend? Don't you ever notice the person who won't really be present when you have a job to rave about or a boyfriend to introduce? But when that boyfriend dumps you or you get fired? Look who pops up in your messages. It's obvious, and yet we all know them. We engage with them, until we realise what's really going on.

Yes, great friends will be there for you when you're going through the mud but greater friends will be your main cheerleaders when things are going amazing in your life. They will support you and encourage you through it all. Those are the keepers. Really pay attention to how people react when you have great news. It's an eye-opener and a clear sign that it might be time to do some sweeping in your life.

Everyone, at some point, deals with negative people. There are always going to be people who will try to put you down, lie to you, judge you, use you or manipulate you. Those insignificant people will sadly always exist, but it doesn't mean you have to let them have an impact on you. YOU decide who to have in your life, who enriches it and who doesn't. This also goes back to trusting your gut and your feelings. You're not always going to get it right when it comes to people but you can try and sift through the red flags and see who's got your best interests at heart.

And if someone happens to hurt you in some way *How dare they! Do you want me to go kick their butts? I'll do it.* If you can, try and take the high road. Decide if it's worth the trouble and the fight. Nine times out of ten it's just a waste of energy and space. Which you don't have time for because you're too busy being awesome.

If someone hurts you, you shouldn't even bother with them anyway. They don't deserve you and your greatness. The older you get, the less bullshit you'll have time for, anyway. And if you're smart, *which I know you are because you're reading this book,* focus on the good people you have in your life, the ones who know you best and who have your back. As the years go by, you'll realise that you don't need many buddies. You'll weed out a lot of them and treasure the few solid friendships that remain. Those are priceless (see chapter on Friendships & Family).

Ultimately, all you can do is look out for yourself. Simply learn from the wrong people you meet along the way and congratulate yourself for the people you were able to cut out for your own happiness. And if there are still some people you're uncertain about or that you're struggling to remove from your life, I'll just leave you with this: anyone making you feel anything less than good about yourself is just not worth it.

What You See Is What You Get

I'll cut straight to the chase on this one. Remember that quote: *"When people tell you who they are, believe them the first time?"* Well, all is said in that sentence. What you see is usually what you get. I didn't understand this until I was dealing with a very surprising and sudden break-up, one I could've maybe seen coming if I had believed what this guy was saying and doing from day one. But, you know, sometimes you don't want to see or hear it, right?

Sometimes, you think you can try to change this person's mind on a specific subject or you choose to ignore all the signs right in front of you that could end up being a problem in a few months' time. Or maybe you think it's all in your head and there isn't a problem. *Most of the time, it's not in your head, folks.* And yes, I'm fully aware this is some form of delusion.

But haven't we all done it? Choosing to ignore red flags because we secretly hope they'll go away. We tell ourselves that they may not have meant to hurt us that one time, maybe they were having a bad day, a bad week or a month. Maybe, he or she will learn from that mistake, apologise and you can all move forward. And of course, in some cases, it works out. Rough patches and mistakes can be mended.

However, you need to observe some patterns of behaviour. Is this person *really* trying to be better? Are they saying a lot, but not doing anything different? Actions speak louder than words. You can tell a lot more about who a person is through what they are doing instead of what they are saying. It's very easy to say a bunch of nice things but people's actions and the effort they make will show you they care. You can keep making excuses for people but it's not a long-term solution, it's just delaying the problem. Those red flags don't just disappear if we ignore them, they become black skies that overshadow and darken everything.

When people tell you who they are, believe them.

This is obviously a very objective way of seeing things. It's never black and white. Our feelings get in the way and blur a lot of things. I like to think I am very good at reading people. I spend a tremendous amount of time watching people's behaviour, everywhere I go – on the tube, in a cafe, in a restaurant, at a party, everywhere. I love it. You can tell a lot by someone's physical behaviour; it's fascinating. It's the same when you start speaking to someone. What's their body language telling you? Is their eye contact strong? What are they actually *saying* as opposed to *doing*?

Again, there is a certain objectivity when we talk to strangers. Things get a little trickier when you start having feelings for someone.

Like I said, I'm very good at reading people but that doesn't mean I haven't misjudged a couple of people along the way and those times were 100 percent because my feelings clouded my first impression. I let myself believe things, even though I could see it wasn't really going as I'd have liked it to.

The 2nd break up I mentioned in the Love chapter was inevitable, simply from the way it started. The guy had told me he wasn't really looking for anything serious but that he liked me. In my head I thought, 'Oh, I'm going to change your mind. You're going to want something more serious after we hang out for a few months and that's how it's going to go.' And for a while, I thought I had convinced him. We were hanging out a lot, doing 'couple' things and I thought we were going somewhere. He had met my Mum, which was a big deal. He was starting to open up and it felt like we were getting to a more stable place, in an actual relationship. Now that I look back, of course, there were signs he was keeping his distance. He never met my friends, I never met his mates, and even though we saw each other regularly, I often had this feeling he wasn't being completely open and honest. After a few months, out of the blue, he ended it.

Understandably, I was upset. What a waste of time the whole thing felt. We were having a great time and I couldn't understand how he would just walk away from that. After a few weeks, I understood that it was never about me. He liked me; he was just not in a place to be with someone seriously, and he had clearly told me that at the very beginning. Fair enough. It's what happened afterwards that could have been avoided.

As you know, a few months later, he popped up again, saying he had made a big mistake and he would love to give us another try. He was ready for something serious nown Now, my decision to take him back surprised me then and still does to this day, I don't know why I did it. For a brief second, he had convinced me that maybe I had been right all along. I knew that he wanted something serious. I wanted to be right. Or maybe I just wanted the relationship not to be a complete waste of time. Who knows! Of course, I'm human and humans aren't not meant to be objective and rational about people, especially when feelings get involved. It's OK to make mistakes. We let our guard down, we open ourselves up to people. We trust. Except this time, even though I took him back, I was more observant. Not only had my trust been challenged with this guy, but I knew the signs now. And sure enough, after just a few weeks, the same patterns came back and I wasn't going to have any of it. I was not going to delude myself into thinking, yet again, that he wanted something serious. Even if he said he did. Sometimes, actions are more obvious. And this time, I was not convinced enough to let him back in.

I knew I deserved certainty, trust, safety and reassurance. And he was not giving any of that. He was a walking red flag who would disappear again at any moment. So I left. I didn't want to be let down again and it was obvious that it was going to happen again if I let it. I did learn a lot from him, though. I learned how to really pay attention and listen to what a person is telling you. It'll save you many disappointments in the future if you can see what is so often displayed right in front of you. Not only will you not be able to change someone, but you also shouldn't want to. If you need them to change, they are not your person. Every person is entitled to their own feelings and ways of living that have nothing to do with you.

People's true colours might not be obvious for a while but there are usually signs, through what is said and done but most importantly through what is not done.

However, and this is a big however, regardless of the moments I have been stung by people who weren't good for me, I've really had to learn to allow the people that really matter in. This has not been an easy task for me, but it's been a necessary one. Because here's the thing: not everyone is going to be shit, guys. If you can get past betrayals and disappointments, you may realise amazing people do exist. And you have to find a way to let them in.

"When people tell you who they are, believe them" also applies to the great people in your life. I know being burned by some makes it difficult to trust again, believe me, I know. But it is possible. Time heals most wounds and hopefully, you can find it in you to rely on the people who actually want what's best for you. Trustworthy people are hard to come by but it is important to open your heart to those who really mean it. If they show you who they are through their meaningful actions, words, presence and support, it's important to allow yourself to trust and believe those people. At some point, you just have to believe that you've become wiser and more in tune with your surroundings and instincts. It's natural to feel guarded after being hurt, however, this does not mean you have to shut out the people that mean well.

A few years after that break-up, I started dating a truly wonderful guy. He was so available to me and showed me he cared in every possible way I could imagine. He was attentive, thoughtful, kind and just really wanted to make me happy. And yet, I was guarded. I was so scared. My parents hadn't actually painted a nice picture of what a good, solid, loving relationship should be and I didn't want to get hurt. I didn't know if I could trust my judgement. I had built walls around me to make sure no one would come in and break it all down. It was a habit and a defence mechanism I had perfected over a lifetime. But being that guarded isn't fulfilling in any way because you're pushing away the good that's coming towards you.

It took this new man calling me out on my bullshit and defensiveness to realise how ridiculous I was being. I was missing out on a lot more by being so guarded, and I couldn't see what was right in front of me: a man who just wanted to make me happy. I needed to shake that off and learn to trust again and be open with him. And trust me, once my guard was down, I found out that the other side of that tough wall is filled with more love, safety and comfort than I could've imagined.

Being blindsided by a person or having your trust broken sucks. It's tough and can take a while to mend. But it doesn't mean all people will be out to hurt you. This was a huge lesson for me. When people SHOW YOU WHO THEY ARE, BELIEVE THEM. When they show their goodness, their vulnerability and their emotions, believe them. The alternative is a lonely, isolated, boring place, where all you've got is the walls around you to keep you warm. *And believe me, walls don't keep you warm.*

Oh and another important point: listen to what your trustworthy peeps tell you from time to time. I can't tell you how many times I've been blown away by the people in my life. Not only do they want what's best for me and have my best interests at heart, but they sometimes know me better than I know myself. It's scary. But it's true.

They've seen something in someone or something that I did not clock at all. They've encouraged me to take a scary step because they knew I needed a push. Letting them do that has taken a minute. I'm quite a stubborn person and I don't like relying on people in general. I used to think I could do it all on my own and that asking for advice or trusting someone with a decision was making me weak. Boy, was I wrong.

You can NOT go through life on your own, listening to your own voice. That doesn't work. You might think it's the safest option because you're being independent and at least you only have yourself to blame if shit hits the fan, but no. People are what matters. You need your people to guide you through life, to help you get up when you've fallen, to help you laugh your way through it all.

Letting people in has been one of the biggest blessings in my life so far. I got tremendously lucky with the friendships and partner I have today (see Friendships chapter). And it's usually all come down to a gut feeling I've had with each and every one of them. But I have had to learn how to listen to what my people have to say, when I'm uncertain, stubborn, not seeing the situation clearly, or simply not being kind to myself. I've learned to take their wise advice. I've learned that if I'm not doing ok, I can rely on them to help me. I can also count on them to tell me the shit I don't want to hear but need to anyway.

If you're anything like me, you're not a huge fan of relying on people. You might like doing things your way and you think you know what's best for you. And of course, sometimes it works. But opening yourself up will create more memorable relationships and moments. Breakthroughs, breakdowns, fits of laughter, trust, being completely yourself, being vulnerable, being HUMAN. Those people will surprise you because turns out, you DON'T always know everything about everything AND they are there for you no matter what. Basically, sometimes just shut up and listen, *to the worthy people of course.*

When people tell you who they are, believe them. When beautiful, encouraging, loving people enter your life, embrace them with all you've got. Sure, you're going to bump into some bad eggs from time to time but USE those instincts we talked about. They will most likely know who is good for you and who isn't. Aside from Mum's crazy friend of course. *There really was no warning there. Even our guts were like 'WTF is going on.'* Trust your gut when it comes to the right people and let those humans in. You'll be much better for it and life will be way more enjoyable with them by your side. People are what matters, so make them matter in your life.

Ultimately, you, and only you, know what's going to make you happiest and you have to lead your life in that manner. You don't want to look back in ten years' time and realise that you went against your instincts and it led you to miss out on something or someone. Ten years from now, make sure you can say that you *chose* your life, you didn't settle for it because of the noise that overshadowed your own voice. You've got a much better chance of living the life you want by listening to your gut.

And in ten years' time, all I can wish is that you did so with a strong peace of mind and real pride in trusting yourself with it. Now, go make some choices!

AUNTY ANGE TIPS

- If it feels wrong, it probably is. You have every right to walk away, no matter the situation.

- What other people think does NOT matter. If something makes you happy, it doesn't have to make sense to others. Just do it.

- Don't be afraid to make mistakes. Just make sure you learn from each one of them.

- If that friend does not cheer you on or celebrate your wins in life, she is not your friend.

- Don't be too hard on yourself. Instincts grow with time and age.

- The only people who matter are the people contributing to your happiness and peace.

- Don't be too stubbornly independent. Listen to your loved ones, hear them out.

Remember when I said to take the high road when someone hurts you? I would say nine times out of ten that's accurate. The tenth time though...knock yourself out if the person deserves a kick in the arse!

RAPID FIRE TIPS

Mostly Embarrassing Things I Have Learned Along the Way.

Let's finish this book with some quick-fire tips from the letter I wrote to myself on my 30th birthday. To be clear, they were all meant for me, but I felt they were wise enough not to share. You're welcome.

- Corn flour is not the same as normal flour, darling. Also, don't ever bake your own birthday cake, for the sake of your friends' health.

- You will have a quarter-life crisis at 25. Don't worry, everyone figures it out eventually. You'll get through it.

- When you hit 28, two-day hangovers will become a thing overnight. No warning, just pain.

- Don't try cooking pasta in a kettle; it doesn't work, breaks the kettle, pisses flatmates off, etc.

- Spend your money on experience and travel, not on stuff.

- But treat yourself.

- If you're not having fun, you can leave. You don't have to explain why, you can just leave.

- Don't compare yourself with others; the only person you should be is yourself.

- Stay calm, you'll get there.

- The entire concept of having it figured out is an illusion made up by people who built a system thinking you should. You have the answer, no one else.

- No answer is an answer.

- Indecision is a decision.

- Hurt people hurt people.

- Stop judging people because they behave differently from you.

- Gut feelings are guardian angels.

- If it costs you your peace, it's too expensive.

- If it's not a hell yes, it's a hell no.

- Stop following the crowd; sit alone if you have to.

- Get a good skin-care routine going. Whether you like it or not, time does pass and your skin will be the first one to tell you that.

- Stop plucking your eyebrows, bushy is back!

- Give your doctor a break. That headache you have is not a tumour, nor is an eye twitch or a bruise. Just give him or her a rest.

- Being perfect is overrated, boring and, frankly, impossible.

- When you feel like crying, do. Let that shit out.

- READ. Read loads of books. Knowledge is power.

- It is not your job to fix people. Let them be.

- Some moments in life are just going to be crap.

- Making the bed is always going to be shit; stop complaining every single time you have to do it.

- Men are a complete mystery, and I am told that this doesn't change after you hit 30. So, that's something to look forward to.

- Some tops do *absolutely* need ironing.

- When you spill something on your clothes, deal with it right away. Don't put it back in the closet and pretend it never happened.

- Your hair will never be big or curly. Leave it ALONE. *This one was mostly for me.*

- Tell your family and friends that you love them; hug them when you can.

Tell yourself that you love yourself. A little self-love goes a long, long way. You are and have always been enough.

Lots of love,

A 30-year-old, wiser, gentler, more protective Angélique. Xx

PS: This whole book was inspired by a letter I wrote to myself, to my younger self, the day I turned 30. I urge you all to do the same. It's a surprising, cathartic and moving journey, that will make you realise how much you've grown, but also how much learning is yet to happen. And who knows, you might even make a book out of it...

ACKNOWLEDGEMENTS

This book would not have made the light of day without the encouragement and support from a few key people. First and foremost, thank you to my mum, the brightest shiny light in my life, thank you for allowing me to tell a few of your stories and always being a constant source of inspiration and admiration for me. Thank you to Simon, my partner in life and love. Thank you for giving me a kick in the butt everytime I was convinced this book was a 'what the fuck was I thinking?' mistake. You pushed me to get this book and my life stories out there and I am so grateful. Thank you to my beautiful girlfriends, Louise, Sara, Adele, Maeva, Jen, Sabrina and Sophie for the tales, the memories, and for being hugely important pillars in my life. Thank you Arielle, Ceri, Reggie, Yaron and PaulD. Thank you to my lovely family, Dad, Antoine, Catherine, Grandad, Mamie, Coralie, Delphine and Kathy to name a few, for supporting me and letting me share my story. I am forever grateful to the lucky stars that brought me all these special people into my life...hopefully they never stop taking my frantic, overly dramatic calls anytime soon.

Love, Ange x

ANGÉLIQUE JOAN

Angélique Joan, an actor and writer, was born in 1990 in Surrey, UK, and was raised on the beautiful coast of Brittany in France. *"Ready, Set, 30: A tale of figuring it all out...whatever that means"* is her writing debut.

After receiving her French literary Baccalaureat, specialising in philosophy and languages, Angélique studied English literature and Drama at Rennes University.

Halfway through her degree, her desire for adventure, love for acting and need to challenge herself took over. She took the plunge by moving to London to pursue that career path while finishing her Master's degree remotely.

In the past decade in London, with a few stints in Los Angeles and New-York to study screenwriting, Angélique's credits in TV and film include BBC Doctors, The Crown and Allied. She also wrote and directed her first short film in 2019 called 'Locked Out', and is currently in the process of producing her TV pilot 'Girls Like Us'.

Printed in Great Britain
by Amazon

85233637R00149